# Transition Skills for
# Post-Secondary Success:
# Reflections for
# High School Students
# with Learning Disabilities

Other books edited by Teresa Allissa Citro

*Parenting the Child with Learning Disabilities:*
*The Experts Speak*

*Successful Lifetime Management:*
*Adults with Learning Disabilities*

# Transition Skills for Post-Secondary Success:

## *Reflections for High School Students with Learning Disabilities*

*edited by*

**Teresa Allissa Citro**
**Executive Director**
**Learning Disabilities Association of Massachusetts**

# Learning Disabilities
# Association of Massachusetts

*This book is dedicated to the most
important men in my life,
my husband, Joseph and son, Justin Noah*

# Contents

# *Foreword*

I recall meeting with a parent one evening in 1973. She was trying to accept the recently received learning disability diagnosis of her 10-year-old son. Understandably anxious and concerned, she asked desperate questions about her son's diagnosis and prognosis. "What about college?" she asked, haltingly.

"I don't like to place limitations on kids," I responded, "but a successful college experience seems unlikely for Sean. But maybe things will change..."

I had no idea how significantly the post-secondary picture *would* change in the coming decades. Thanks to groundbreaking legislation and pioneering educators, high school is no longer the end of the educational road for students with learning problems. College and post-secondary training are now realities and achievable goals for many special education students.

However, the road to post-secondary education is not well paved; it contains detours, roadblocks and potholes that students and parents must consider. This latest LDAM publication provides a road map and some sage advice from individuals who have traveled that road. The articles, essays and chapters provide pragmatic and useful information — and a dose of inspiration, as well.

This book is, largely, about transition. My experience in special education as a teacher and administrator has taught me that transitions are invariably difficult and challenging for students with learning disabilities. Small transitions (i.e., shifting from the reading lesson to recess in the elementary school) create small anxieties. Large transitions (i.e., moving from middle school to high school) create large anxieties. Therefore, transitions large and small must be carefully planned and choreographed. *Transition Skills for Post-Secondary Success: Reflections for High School Students with Learning Disabilities* will be of great help in the planning of one of life's most significant transitions.

Today, post-secondary options abound for high school students with a leaning problem. But each of those students owes a debt of gratitude to the students who came before them. The college world was quite skeptical about the ability of learning disabled students to perform successfully in post-secondary settings. Their skepticism was allayed by the hard work, effort and success of the pioneering group of students with learning problems who attended college in the 1980s. They proved that learning disabled students have the determination, drive and devotion to effectively handle college level curricula.

These courageous and goal-directed young people followed the sage advice of the Native American proverb:

> "Go not upon the well beaten path. Rather go where no path yet exists
> and leave a trail for others."

*Richard D. Lavoie,*

President
Riverview School

# *Acknowledgments*

The Learning Disabilities Association of Massachusetts would like to thank Mitchell College, New London, Connecticut for its generous grant to fund the publication of this book. Without their support, *Transition Skills for Post-Secondary Success: Reflections for High School Students with Learning Disabilities*, would not exist.

It was a pleasure to work with people who often knew better than I did myself what it was that I wanted this project to be. Special thanks go to my friend, Moira Anne Munns for numerous hours of editorial assistance; thanks to Michelle D'Agostino for help with the art design of the cover and for always giving me exactly what I'm looking for; thanks to Joe Brownstein and Bill Crabtree of Waltham Printing Services, Inc., Waltham, Massachusetts for extending themselves to do our printing; thanks to M. Shelley Finn not only for typesetting/layout, but also for lending her editorial eye and providing meaningful suggestions.

The foreword of Rick Lavoie, President, Riverview School, East Sandwich, Massachusetts conveys our message of hope. I appreciate the kind encouragement and support he has always given to me and to LDAM.

The authors, Marsha A. Glines, Ph.D., Leslie S. Goldberg, M.Ed., CEP, Barbara Priddy Guyer, Ed.D., Rosa A. Hagin, Ph.D., HEATH Resource Center, Doris J. Johnson, Ph.D., Frank Kline, Ph.D., Bart Pisha, Ed.D., Charles E. Rehberg, Ed.D., Maureen K. Riley, M.Ed., William J. Rowley, Ed.D., Roxanne Ruzic, M.Ed. understand the transition skills required for academic success in college and how difficult it is for students with learning disabilities to acquire or sometimes even identify these essential skills. They have shared my desire of bringing this important information to students and their families. The sensitive, insightful and instructive contributions of these authors will influence and benefit the lives of many young people.

Finally, I must thank the Board of Directors of the Learning Disabilities Association of Massachusetts for whom I have the greatest respect. They are: Presidents, Jane Derman-Kilgallon and Maureen Riley, Vice President, Jerome Schultz, Lizanne Campbell, Ruth and Lee Glazerman, Larry Kotin, Michelle Pastore, Stephen Rothenberg, Howard Shane, Robin Welch and Lorraine Zimmerman. Their dedication to disseminating information and improving the lives of those with learning disabilities is heroic. As time passes and our work together continues, my admiration increases. I look forward to many years of collaboration to ensure that each student with learning disabilities meets with success.

# *Preface*

High School is typically the time in students' lives when they must make the choices that will set them on their paths to future vocations, education and careers. They must bring their goals, dreams and desires into focus as they make these difficult decisions. For the average student this process sometimes feels stressful and overwhelming. For the student with learning disabilities it may seem insurmountable. This book, *Transition Skills for Post-Secondary Success: Reflections for High School Students with Learning Disabilities*, is intended to be a tool in the post-secondary planning "toolbox." It was written to assist students with learning disabilities. With this book and the help of parents and professionals who work with students with learning disabilities, these students will be able to reach their goals, see their dreams and achieve their desires.

The contributors to this project lend their expertise to provide essential information to high school students and the adults in the lives of these students. There are methods and mechanisms to support students at every step in the process of preparing for, applying to and attending college. Knowing what the supports are and how to utilize them, will permit students to make informed choices. Everyone has strengths as well as weaknesses. Each author describes the measures to take to minimize the effect of weaknesses and to highlight the special talents and gifts that students with learning disabilities bring to the college experience.

Guidance counselors and other professionals who work with students who have learning disabilities must keep in mind that you may be the only people guiding them through this decision making process. Although it is necessary to be realistic, it is unfair to limit these students because of our expectations. If the student's aspirations are high and our expectations are low, perhaps what is required is that we modify our expectations. Often students are dissuaded from pursuing a particular career or course of study because of their disabilities. What a loss for students, for our society and for us if we focus on what they cannot do at the expense of recognizing what they can do. It is our responsibility to encourage students to be all that they can be

Students reading this book need to remember never to give up on your dreams. The route to your success may not be direct. Use the information here to help you explore the academic support services of institutions of higher education. Select a college or university whose programs and services can meet your needs. Success is possible. Everyone despite their learning style can reach their full potential in life.

You have my every good wish for a rewarding career.

*Teresa Allissa Citro*

# Chapter One

# Understanding Your Learning Disabilities

*Doris J. Johnson, Ph.D.*
*Northwestern University*

**Doris J. Johnson, Ph.D.**

Adolescence is a special time in life. Some people might say it is the "best of times and the worst of times" because of the ups and downs, the excitement, and the frustrations that adolescents may feel at home, in school or in social groups. During the adolescent years, you will change in many ways. You will change physically and emotionally. Your thinking and attitudes are also likely to change. You may form new opinions about people and events in the world. In many respects, you will become your own person. The expectations for you at home and at school will also change. Even though you have probably had jobs to do around the house, your parents may begin to expect more of you. In school, you will be expected to do more on your own, to plan your time, and take more difficult courses. At the beginning of adolescence, people will call you "boys and girls" and at the end of this time, you will be "men and women." You will become more independent, and, at the end of adolescence, some of you will be working full time or part-time, and others will be in college or in a vocational training school.

Some adolescents find these years to be difficult because of their learning disabilities. Even though they are aware that certain things are hard to do, they may not really understand what the term learning disability means. Young people may have mixed feelings about whether they want help for their difficulties and whether they even want to talk about their challenges. Some students are embarrassed to go for tutoring. Others accept their problems and want to take action. Often these concerns and feelings are not new because most learning disabilities are identified in elementary or middle school. However, some students may not be tested or identified until adolescence or even adulthood if their learning disabilities are mild, if they have the ability to compensate for their weaknesses, or if tutors are provided.

Whether the problems were identified in early childhood or not, adolescents frequently want to know more about their learning disabilities, what the terms mean, what can be done about the problems, and what types of schools or jobs they should consider. The purpose of this chapter is to present the questions that adolescents ask us, and to discuss some issues that may be of concern to you.

*What is a learning disability?*

Many people do not understand the meaning of the term "learning disability." This confusion is not unusual because the term encompasses many types of problems. Not everyone has the same sort of difficulty. For example, some people have trouble reading, but others have math or listening comprehension problems. Some students have only one or two concerns whereas others have weaknesses in many areas of achievement. Students may have mild, moderate or severe problems.

Sometimes people think that a person with a learning disability is unable to learn or make progress. This is not true. We have seen many adults who improved basic skills in reading, writing, oral communication, mathematics and other areas of weakness (Johnson & Blalock, 1987).

All students with learning disabilities have strengths as well as weaknesses. Usually they have more strengths than weaknesses, and most adolescents can explain

2

what is easy or difficult for them. For example, some say they have difficulty taking notes in class, or reading or writing. They describe the problems they have in paying attention in noisy classrooms. Others talk about the problems they have had in making or keeping friends, in learning to drive, or in making change when they go to a store. Most also can list the things they can do well. They may say that they are good listeners, that they like to read, that they are good in math or that they have good friends, but they can not spell or write themes. Because not everyone has the same problem, it is sometimes hard to find someone to talk with about your difficulties, but usually you can share some common experiences with people who are close to you.

People with learning disabilities have many strengths. They are alike because they can hear and see, and they have average to above average intelligence. They do not have physical or motor handicaps, but some have minor coordination or balance problems. They do not have severe emotional problems, but they may lack confidence because of frustrations and concerns about their school work and achievement. They usually want to learn, but they have problems processing certain types of information that may interfere with listening, speaking, reading, writing, mathematics or reasoning. For example, they may have auditory memory problems that interfere with their ability to learn language or follow directions. Others have trouble remembering math facts or spelling words. Others have nonverbal communication problems and difficulty interpreting the meaning of facial expressions, body language or tone of voice.

A learning disability can occur with other problems such as Attention Deficit Disorder, but not everyone with ADD has a learning disability. People with ADD or ADHD have trouble focusing and maintaining attention. They are often impulsive and poorly organized. Doctors may prescribe medication for ADD, but not LD.

Sometimes, people have emotional problems as well as learning disabilities. When this is the case they may need specialists to help them with their feelings as well as learning difficulties. In this chapter the emphasis is on specific learning disabilities.

**What are the symptoms or types of problems adolescents with LD might have?**

Listening Comprehension

Peole with listening comprehension problems hear, but they may have difficulty understanding or remembering language they hear. It probably feels a little like being in a foreign country when you do not understand the language. Some students are confused by words that sound similar. For example, one adolescent thought that the words "muscle" and "muzzle" sounded the same. Another thought that "biography" and "bibliography" were the same.

Other students have no difficulty hearing the differences between words, but they have problems understanding. All of us hear words we do not understand in new courses or unfamiliar situations. People who are unfamiliar with sports may be confused by words they hear in a radio or TV broadcast of an athletic event. Others do not understand computer language. However, some people with learning disabilities have difficulty understanding words they have heard their parents, teachers and peers use many times. Sometimes this is because words are used so quickly that they do not have time to process the meaning. Many also have difficulty understanding words that have several meanings, such as "check," "bill" or "pack." The English language has many words with multiple meanings. In school, the same words may have different meanings in the different courses you take. The word "symbol" has different meanings in language, in mathematics, chemistry, music and psychology. Abstract words such as "liberty" or "justice" are often difficult to understand, as are idioms or figures of speech which are used in literature and in many social situations. For example, a teenager who heard "the girl was met with icy stares" thought that it meant the girl might fall because the stairs were slippery. She did not understand that the sentence meant someone was staring at her in a stern (cold) manner. Jokes and humor may also be difficult to comprehend. Students with these problems need to ask for help when they need it and to ask teachers about the vocabulary that is most important in class.

Students with language problems often have difficulty understanding lectures or long discussions in class. And, because writing is often hard, they cannot take good notes. In these cases, students may find it helpful to use a tape recorder in class so they can listen to the discussion again. Most teachers are willing to help if they know what is difficult for you. It is important that you tell your teachers what you did not understand. Special educators may help you get accommodations and review the material that was discussed in class.

Many people with learning disabilities have short term auditory memory problems so they cannot remember directions in school or at work. If you have such a problem, it is a good idea to ask the speaker to repeat the directions, try to rehearse, say them to yourself or write them down. One of the major purposes of writing is to aid memory. Many people make lists, keep a diary or put important information into computers so they do not have to worry about remembering everything. One adolescent told us he always kept a small notebook in his pocket so he could write things he needed to remember.

Oral Expressive Language and Speaking

Many adolescents with learning disabilities have good listening comprehension, but they have trouble expressing their ideas clearly. Sometimes this is because they have difficulty remembering words they want to say. The words are "on the tip of the tongue," but they cannot recall them. This usually happens with names, places and very specific words. When you are called on to give the name of an author or the capital of a country, you may not be able to remember the name quickly. When this happens, it is sometimes helpful to give an explanation to show that you understand. Occasionally, teachers will help by giving you multiple choice questions. As with other memory problems, anxiety or worry makes it more difficult to remember things. Therefore, we suggest that students try to remain calm if they have word retrieval difficulty. Sometimes, it is helpful to try "mental search strategies." When you cannot recall a word, try to think of the first sound or create a picture of the word in your mind. Writing important words that you need to remember will also strengthen recall.

Adolescents with learning disabilities also may have difficulty organizing their thoughts to give an oral summary or presentation in class. They are slow to recall words, to formulate complete sentences and to organize their thoughts. In order to improve, it might be helpful to practice a summary before you go to class or ask your teachers for suggestions.

Some students also have problems carrying on a conversation. Unfortunately, some listeners interrupt or do not wait for you to express your ideas. This can be frustrating. Even if it is hard for you to express your ideas, you can learn to be a good listener. When someone else is talking, watch the speaker, and do not interrupt. Listening to others and showing that you care can be a real strength.

Remember that not everyone with a learning disability has problems with oral language. Sometimes it is a strength. When this is the case, students may be permitted to give oral reports or take oral examinations instead of writing.

Reading

Many people with learning disabilities have difficulty reading, but not all poor readers have learning disabilities. Some poor readers have not had good instruction; others do not want to read. In contrast, most people with learning disabilities want to read, but they cannot sound out the words or comprehend as well as their classmates. Others are very slow readers so they tire quickly.

The term you may have heard for reading disability is "dyslexia," which usually means a problem in recognizing or "sounding out" unfamiliar words. In the past, people thought that dyslexics reversed letters and words. This is sometimes true, but most studies now show that they have problems reading unfamiliar words. Often they have difficulty breaking words into syllables or sounds, and blending them together. When this is the case, reading comprehension will be weak. In other words, if you cannot recognize a word, it is difficult to get to the meaning. Many dyslexics, however, use context and try to get the "gist" of the passage by reading around the difficult words. This helps sometimes, but if you are asked to read words in lists or in a phone book, there is no context. Dyslexics, like other people with learning disabilities, often need special services because they cannot teach themselves to read. In addition, they usually need help with spelling. If you cannot read words, it is unlikely that you can spell them. But the spelling problems vary. Certain dyslexics can "hear" or process all of the sounds and syllables in words, but they cannot remember how certain parts of words look. Therefore, they may write "instatoot" instead of "institute." They also have difficulty with homonyms (words that are spelled differently, but sound the same). These include words such as "their," "there" and "they're" or "serial" and "cereal" and many others. Other dyslexics tend to omit sounds and syllables. They may write "instut" for "institute." Although spell checks on computers can be of help, they do not catch all of the mistakes. Therefore, students might need a tutor and learn how to spell "demon" words that they need to write often.

Reading, of course, requires more than word recognition. It requires comprehension. Certain students with learning disabilities can recognize or sound out (decode) words, but they do not understand the meaning. Sometimes this is because of the listening comprehension problems discussed above. If we do not understand words we hear, we will probably not be able to understand them when we read. On the other hand, reading comprehension is sometimes easier, than listening because you can review the words in print. Listening requires more auditory memory than reading.

Other people with poor reading comprehension do not use good strategies. They try to remember everything they read, or they just skim for the main points. Sometimes skimming is a good idea, but at other times we need to read carefully to get the meaning and to make inferences. Some students understand the facts and literal meanings, but they do not interpret the ideas correctly. Students with these problems should ask for help in order to develop better reading strategies. Note taking, summarizing, and self-questioning strengthen comprehension. Highlighting and underlining are not enough to understand what you read.

Finally, many adolescents and adults with learning disabilities are slow readers. They comprehend if given enough time, but cannot complete work in a timely manner. Often they need to read and re-read in order to remember and comprehend. If evaluative test results indicate this problem, students may be given time accommodations. More time helps many students.

Writing

Most students who have oral language and reading problems have some type of written language difficulty. This is because writing is built on other, more basic language skills. Sometimes adolescents still struggle with handwriting, quick letter formation and spacing. While these are not the most important aspects of writing, students may want to improve these basic skills. The problems presented by the lack of mastery of the mechanical aspects of writing can be avoided with use of the computer. However, certain visual-spatial-motor problems may also interfere with keyboarding. Nevertheless, papers written on the computer are usually more legible and easier to proofread for mistakes.

As stated above, many students have difficulty spelling. Others have problems organizing themes, research papers or book reports. Sometimes this is because they have difficulty doing the reading and research for the paper. Others find it hard to get started, to organize their ideas, to revise and edit. Writing is hard work. Even great writers talk about the time it takes to organize, revise and edit their work. Because people with learning disabilities may have difficulty with reading, vocabulary, grammar, spelling and organization, writing is particularly difficult. Therefore, you may need to start on your projects long before they are due so that you have time to revise and edit.

You may find that you make many "unexpected" mistakes when you write. Students with learning disabilities tend to omit little words or word endings so their written work has many mistakes. The grammar check on the computer may be helpful, but it is not fool-proof. Therefore, it may be necessary to learn how to detect your own mistakes. Shaughnessy (1977) said that college students who are poor writers need to learn to read like proofreaders, checking each word and sentence very carefully. Adolescents and college students with learning disabilities need to do the same thing or ask someone to edit papers before turning them in to the teacher.

Mathematics

Some, but not all, students with learning disabilities, have difficulty with mathematics. Often they cannot remember math facts quickly, in which case, a calculator should be used whenever possible. Others have difficulty remembering procedures for certain types of problems. For example, Johnson & Blalock (1987) found adults had trouble with fractions, decimals and percentages. Some said they had never learned the procedures, but others said they forgot. If you have any of these problems, it is a good idea to "brush up" on these procedures since fractions, decimals and percentages are needed for many daily activities such as making change, measuring or estimating the cost of something you want to buy.

Sometimes students have difficulty using measuring tools such as rulers, compasses or speedometers. Even reading a thermometer or telling time is difficult for some people. Special educators will work with you on these skills if necessary.

Students with language disorders may have difficulty with the vocabulary and complex sentences used in mathematics, algebra or geometry. We suggest they check with a high school adviser to decide which level mathematics courses are most appropriate. Sometimes we recommend a basic math or business math course to make sure that students will be able to handle their personal finances and budgets.

In certain cases, mathematics is a strength. Several famous scientists who had reading or language difficulties said they had very good mathematics skills. But, poor readers may not be able to read the story problems. If necessary, you can ask someone to read the problems to you.

Reasoning and Problem Solving

Students with learning disabilities may also have difficulty with certain types of problem solving. For example, they may have trouble organizing plans for a trip, preparing a meal or completing complex school tasks such as writing a research paper, which require several steps and organization of ideas. If you have such problems, using preplanning strategies may help. Make check lists, prioritize your activities and think through problems carefully.

Social Skills

Some adolescents with learning disabilities have very good social skills. They have friends and are in many activities. Others, however, wonder why they have such difficulty making and keeping friends. We emphasize "some," because many students with learning disabilities are outgoing, and have excellent interpersonal skills. Others, however, have trouble understanding language, slang and the rapid speech of their peers. Therefore, it is difficult for them to keep up with group conversations. They do not know how to carry on a good conversation and say they cannot think of questions to ask people. Therefore, they find it hard to be a part of a group. Some say they are lonely, and want to learn how to make and keep friends.

Other students have problems with nonverbal communication. They do not always notice or interpret facial expressions, body language, or the tone of voice, and cannot tell whether someone is being sarcastic or funny. Certain schools have special programs to help students improve their social skills. Teachers may use role playing and other techniques for practice.

Most adolescents want to participate in activities outside the classroom. We suggest you choose things that are fairly easy for you so you can use your talents and strengths. Sometimes athletics is a strength. Famous athletes have talked about their learning disabilities and inspired many young people. Other adolescents are good in art. We have seen many poor readers who are fine painters and photographers. Some have used these talents when they chose an occupation or job. Pat Buckley Moss, a fine painter, has talked about her dyslexia at L.D.A. meetings. Other people with learning disabilities have musical talents, but they may have problems reading music. If they have teachers who understand their weaknesses, they may help students choose an appropriate instrument and find the best way to learn. Many students with learning disabilities do volunteer work, helping with city clean up jobs, assisting in day care centers or homes for the elderly. Being kind to others is a real strength for many people who have learning disabilities.

### If I don't understand my problems, whom should I talk to?

Many people with learning disabilities have problems understanding their learning disabilities. This could be because adults have not explained the problems clearly, or because the words that professional people use are confusing. If this is the case, talk to your parents, teachers, counselors, doctor or someone who knows and understands you. It is often helpful to make a list of your questions or concerns before scheduling an appointment. If you have trouble understanding the explanations, ask for a chart or list of your strengths and weaknesses. Having that information in writing may be helpful so you can review it later on your own.

### What kind of tests are used to diagnose a learning disability and what do the results mean?

If you have never had an evaluation or if you need new test results, you may want to find out about the kinds of tests that people will give you. All students have taken group achievement tests in school, but the tests for learning disabilities are given individually by psychologists or special educators. Generally, you will be given several different kinds of tests; some will require oral language, reading, writing or mathematics. Some tests will be nonverbal, such as puzzles and mazes. Some tests will be timed; others will be untimed.

Many tests are needed to see whether you have a learning disability. It is necessary to get information about your overall mental ability (intelligence) and achievement in the areas discussed above, and to explore your ability to process and remember various types of information. Some tests are timed in order to evaluate your speed of processing. Students may do well on untimed reading or writing tests, but poorly on those that are timed. If this is the case, you may be able to ask for more time on your examinations in school.

If you get an evaluation, someone will also talk to you and your parents about your health, early development and school history. They will want to know when you first started having difficulty and what kinds of help you have had. They will want to know about your early schooling and how you were taught to read, write and calculate. Someone may also do a social  history to learn more about your interests, hobbies and social activities.  All of this background information is helpful to determine why students have learning difficulties.

After the testing is completed, someone will talk to you and/or your family about the results and the kind of help that is needed.  In public schools an Individual Educational Program including goals will be written and discussed with your parents or guardians.  Students over 14 years of age may be included in these discussions.

*What kinds of help are available?  When and where will the help be given?*

The types of help that you are able to get will depend upon your problems and the services that are available in your school.  Almost all schools and colleges will arrange for accommodations if the test results show that you have a disability.  An accommodation means that assignments, tests and other things will be arranged so that you have the chance to show what you know, or to make sure information is presented in a way that you are able to understand.  For example, people who cannot read very much will have a hard time reading textbooks, so they might be able to have tape recorded textbooks or someone who will read the books to them.  Some students will get special accommodations such as extra time on tests, a tape recorder for lecture notes, a reader, a note taker, a computer to take notes, and in some cases, different types of exams.  You might be able to take oral instead of written exams, or multiple choice instead of essay questions.  It depends on your test results, as well as the suggestions from the teachers.  You and your family can decide whether you want to accept these accommodations.

Other students will receive direct help on vocabulary, reading, writing, math, study strategies and other weaknesses.  This means that a teacher will work with you on word meanings, reading skills, spelling, problem solving or anything else that is difficult for you.  Often, they help adolescents develop better strategies for completing assignments, particularly big projects and papers.  The services may be in the regular classroom or in a learning center or in a resource room, either individually or with a few other students.  Sometimes students are enrolled in special levels of classes with others who have learning difficulties.

Families sometimes decide to have private evaluations rather than testing in school.  If you had private testing outside the school, you will need to share the test results with your teachers and principal in order to get accommodations and support.  This is hard for some students because they do not want to admit they have a learning disability, or they would rather not tell anyone about their problem.  The decision is up to you and your parents, but, in the end, most students want the help.

Some families choose private schools or tutoring.  Certain private schools for learning disabilities give extra help on reading and other skills.  In other cases, students stay in their regular class and get tutoring after school from a special teacher.

Many students find it hard to talk about their problems with other people.  Adolescents, in particular, find it difficult because they want very much to be included in social groups and think that they might not be accepted if they have a disability.  Just remember, a learning disability, like other kinds of handicaps, will not interfere with all of your activities. Many people will not even know you have a problem. Learning disabilities are "hidden" handicaps. You cannot really see that the person has a problem as you can with someone who has a physical handicap. Learning disabilities show up only when people are asked to listen, speak, read, write, calculate or perform tasks that require skills they have not been able to learn at home or in the regular classroom. You do not have to talk with people about your problems, but students sometimes find it is a relief to simply explain what things are hard. If you do talk about your difficulty, use simple language, and say that you have a problem remembering what you hear, or problems with reading and spelling. Then people will understand why you need tutoring or special accommodations.

On the other hand, some adolescents may want to discuss their feelings with a counselor, a social worker or psychologist. These may be available in schools or in private settings.

Students often ask whether they will get over their learning disability. Most make progress, but some weaknesses may remain. That is why many colleges now have special programs.

### Should I consider college?

The decisions about college will need to be made with you, your parents, teachers and advisers. You need to think about whether you want to continue in school or get a job. Sometimes students work for a while and then go back to school part time. Others go on to college or vocational training programs. Many colleges and universities now have support systems for students with handicaps. In addition, many schools have transition programs that will help with the move to school or work. Most high schools have guidance counselors who will give you information about schools and jobs. Public libraries also have resource materials.

Many students with learning disabilities can go to college, but they should choose schools carefully. They should think about the size, the location, the cost of the schools and the types of support they offer. Sometimes it is a good idea to begin college with a light load of courses so that you have time to complete all of the work. If you take a full load, you might choose classes that do not require too many skills related to your weaknesses. For example, if you have a reading or writing problem, find out how many books and papers are required in each course. Then, if you can, you might be able to take at least some classes that require less reading and writing. It is better to do well and feel successful than to be overwhelmed with work that cannot be completed.

### What kinds of work do people with LD do?

Many of you may wonder about future work. As with all of us, this depends upon interests, ability, skills and education. People with learning disabilities are in all walks of life, but generally, they choose occupations in which they can use their strengths. We know doctors, lawyers, business people, teachers, special educators, artists, musicians, waitresses, postmen, plumbers, grocers, farmers, landscapers, maids, pet shop owners and many others with learning disabilities who are working around us every day. When you begin thinking about work, it is a good idea to consider all of the skills that are needed for a particular job. The person with poor mathematics skills should probably not choose jobs that require rapid, accurate calculation. The person with a writing problem should think about occupations that require other types of skills.

Sometimes people need help with interviews, applications and job coaching. It takes some people longer to learn how to perform certain skills, but once they learn, most do well. However, when things are not going well, it may be helpful to talk to a boss or supervisor about problems and needs. It is important to make certain that you get to work on time, that you put forth good effort, and do your best. If the work is too stressful, you might consider a change. Vocational counselors may help you select jobs that are related to your interests and strengths.

*What do people mean when they talk about self advocacy?*

In recent years, people with learning disabilities have been encouraged and taught how to advocate for themselves. Since parents and teachers may not always be around to intervene or support you, it is important to learn how to ask for help when you need it. Students are often hesitant to request extra time and help, but in the end, they will benefit by doing so. They need to learn how to request help. If students do not understand a lecture, it is not a good idea to tell the teacher you did not comprehend *anything* in the lesson. It is better to be specific and try to explain what you did not understand. Be tactful and polite.

Sometimes self advocacy will be needed at work. If you are working in a noisy environment, you might request a quieter location or shorter, more frequent breaks. Some people need a little more job coaching and supervision when they begin. Most employers will give more if they realize you will be conscientious and try to do your best.

*Where can I learn more about Learning Disabilities?*

Adolescents and others with learning disabilities often want information, something to read or stories about people who coped and compensated for their weaknesses. Sometimes there are support groups in schools or communities where people share their experiences. You may also want to consider books such as *Different is not Bad* by Sally Smith (1994) who directs a special school, or *Succeeding with LD* by Jill Lauren (1997), an LD teacher who collected stories from adolescents and adults. At the beginning of the book, Lauren says that we will meet some amazing people and if you read her book, you will. All of them found school difficult and sometimes frustrating. At times they felt as if they were stupid, yet they knew deep down that they were not. Students tell their best and worst memories. Most of them say you need to work hard, stay in school, respect others and yourself. The book has stories about people who are good in art, in dance, in science, in teaching, in medicine, business and many other fields. If you read this book, and others like it, the stories may inspire you and help you face some of the difficult times you may experience.

Many people with learning disabilities are strong and resilient. This means that they are able to "bounce back" after their difficulties. We also found that most adults were also very persistent; they kept trying to reach their goals even when the work was hard. This takes effort, courage and physical stamina. Because of this effort and extra work, it is important that you take time to rest and have a good time. Many adults with learning disabilities tell us how much they love nature and the out-of-doors. Others enjoy sports or movies. Find something you like to do and take time to relax.

Remember that everyone finds certain kinds of tasks or school subjects are harder than others. You are not alone. Some find it helpful to join a support group to talk about strategies others have used to cope and compensate for similar weaknesses. These groups are also opportunities to meet and make new friends. Other people want to talk about their problems in private with a counselor, advisor or an understanding teacher. Sometimes talking about your concerns can relieve you of worries so that you can concentrate on your work. Lauren (1997) concludes her book with several ways to succeed with LD. She suggests finding resources and strategies that work for you, keep trying and believe in yourself.

# Chapter Two

# Work Smarter, Not Harder: Develop a Strategic Mindset in High School for College

*Maureen K. Riley, M.Ed.*

**Maureen K. Riley, M.Ed.**

14

During a discussion about succeeding, a student asked, *"What's it all about, Professor?"*
Nobel Prize Laureate, Seamus Heaney answered in his spare, direct way: *"It's all about—getting started, keeping going, and getting started again."*

Purpose

The advice of Seamus Heaney helps put into plain language some of the most complicated ideas in the field of education and, in particular, in special education. All of these apparently simple behaviors—getting started, keeping going, and getting started again—have deep and important underpinnings that need to be understood for the success of students with learning disabilities. Many students with learning disabilities have trouble doing their work:

Getting started: *focusing/analyzing the task/initiating*
  • figuring out and comprehending what is involved in the task
  • deciding what the first move will be
Keeping going: *self-monitoring/ reflecting/ recalling/ sustaining attention/ persisting*
  • holding onto the parts of the problem
  • calling up from memory what is needed to solve the problem
  • juggling all of the pieces needed to complete the work
Getting started again: *shifting attention/ analyzing/ changing course*
  • moving to the next step or stage
  • deciding whether to switch an approach
  • judging when to stop and how begin again

Underlying these seemingly uncomplicated behaviors are multifaceted concepts: attention, memory, task analysis, self-regulation, executive function. These are highly complex ideas requiring continued study and still considered by researchers to be '...unwieldy with fuzzy conceptual boundaries' (Lyon & Krasnegor, 1996, p. xv.).

The existing research has, however, identified and demonstrated that there are particular coping mechanisms central to these concepts which can be critically important to the academic achievement of students with learning disabilities. They have also been shown to be well within reach of students with learning disabilities to develop (Boudah, Schumaker, & Deshler, 1997). These coping mechanisms include metacognition, reflection, self-monitoring, strategizing and planning (Montague, 1998; Swanson, Carson, & Saches-Lee, 1996; Scruggs & Mastropieri, 1993; Wong, 1999).

The goal of this chapter is to unpack and share some of those concepts and coping mechanisms which the research has demonstrated to be most beneficial to students with learning disabilities.

**Quick Tips versus Reliable Resources**

Why is it so important to know what the research says? Quick tips and advice are readily available as solutions for the complex difficulties facing students with learning disabilities (LD). Tips or suggestions may, or may not be, appropriate for an individual student, and loss of time and increased frustration are risks. Interpreting lack of student accomplishment as laziness, procrastination, stubbornness and applying pressure to solve the problem also are not very productive and can be harmful.

When seeking advice it is wise to turn to persons who have devoted lifetimes to the study of how students with learning disabilities learn most effectively. There is a body of knowledge developed by groups of experts in the field of special education based upon research studies—rigorous thinking, planning and intervention—going into the classroom and testing out—what works. The studies extend for several years or longer on a particular topic, for example, to learn about a type of memory process problematic to many students with learning disabilities or about the effectiveness of a specific approach to improve reading comprehension.

**Joining the Professional Dialogue**

Parents and students need to be "let in on" professional dialogue about the advances in the field of special education. Parents so commonly express their frustration with the professional information and terminology used in their children's diagnostic testing reports:

> At the end of the report, metacognitive strategies are recommended. After only a half-hour explanation of all of the different testing, I definitely left not knowing what 'metacognitive' means. I'm not even sure about how the term 'strategy' works. The recommendations listed books full of strategies, and I'm not sure where to begin to help my son.

This man and his son could benefit greatly from understanding these terms, metacognition and strategic problem solving, which have been demonstrated to relate to increased achievement for students with learning disabilities (Swanson et al., 1996). Some authorities in the field of special education go so far as to say that the skills involved in metacognition and strategic problem solving—that is, "...the student's degree of 'know how' including how to study and analyze academic subjects, self-knowledge, confidence and awareness"—are more reliable predictors for college success than even reading or language skills (Greenwood, 1983, p. 241).

**Unpacking some of the Complicated Ideas**

In my experience working with students with learning disabilities and their families, I have found that both parents and students express that they feel empowered and relieved to find that they are clearly able to comprehend and make use of the important concepts, terminology, issues and problems in the field of special education—in particular, the best practices supported by research. The goal here is to share the findings from research in order to combat the disheartening maxim, "...twenty years from research to the real world."

Overview

Strategic Mindset

This chapter develops the components of a *strategic mindset* which the research has identified to be associated with increased achievement for students with learning disabilities.

To develop a *strategic mindset*, the students need to work on:

16

- becoming more self-aware: thinking about their own thinking, knowing about knowing and knowing about memory
- understanding the school environment in which they have to cope
- strategizing and implementing: learning about strategies; trying out, comprehending, and revising strategies to make them work personally for them; experiencing that persistence pays off
- self-monitoring: self-alerting to make use of the strategies when needed; to initiate, to reflect and be selective about which strategy to apply
- reflecting and planning: checking how they are doing, when to keep going and sustain their efforts, and when to stop and see that they need to shift direction
- knowing how and when to ask for help and realizing that appropriate help increases independence

## The Need for Strategic Mindset

Too many students with learning disabilities unnecessarily lack a clear and functional understanding of their learning disabilities (Silver, 2000; Riley, 1999b). Compared to their peers without learning disabilities, they also tend to have a less certain understanding of academic strategies (McPhail & Stone, 1995; Swanson, 1990). They tend to overestimate their own strategic functioning; teachers and other evaluators rate them at a lower level than they rate themselves in this area (Graham, Schwartz, & MacArthur, 1993; Meltzer et al., 1998). To develop the knowledge and skills for a strategic mindset requires serious effort, but putting in the work has high payoff (Boudah et al., 1997).

This chapter is best read by parents and students together. It is not a quick, one-time read. Each citation makes available to the student and parents data-supported information from the years of work by authorities in the field mentioned above. The concepts need to be revisited over time as students work on developing the components encompassed in the term, *strategic mindset*. Taking into consideration the student's age and developmental level in the conversation, even students as young as middle school can begin to become knowledgeable about themselves and the factors affecting their learning, and certainly, high school students have the capacity to become highly informed.

## Practical Information

Included in the appendices and in the text is practical information, such as required college preparatory course sequences; standardized testing requirements for college admissions; SAT, ACT, AP; book list to prepare for standardized tests; questions to ask guidance counselors; student self-evaluations for self-advocacy and self-awareness; listings of potential academic accommodations and technological aids.

## Part I    Self-Knowledge: Appreciating and Trusting Intellectual Strengths
*Getting Rid of the Misunderstandings*

In order to develop the "self-knowledge" and the "know-how" which influence academic success, it is necessary for students with learning disabilities (LD) to realize that it is not a lack of intellectual ability that makes schoolwork more time-consuming and frustrating for them than for their peers. Students need to be reminded that, to be tested and categorized as"LD," they have already demonstrated through diagnostic testing that they are of average or above average intelligence. "The term does not include children who have learning problems which are primarily the result of...mental retardation, or emotional disturbance." (USOE, 1977, p. 65083). The intellectual strength is there for students with LD to be academically successful, to know themselves as learners, to develop the "know how" and, importantly, to reduce the frustration.

The typical battery of tests given to diagnose learning disabilities is a valuable resource to establish this understanding. Too often, however, the disability areas, the weaknesses, become the focus of attention. Because the definition of learning disabilities is so individual and varied, it is not surprising that students with LD do not easily gain a clear grasp of their learning abilities or disabilities (Field, 1996; Lichtenstein, 1993).

Presently, there are intense professional arguments about the definition of LD, but the category of learning disabilities was established for very important reasons which students with LD need to appreciate. One reason was to clarify serious misunderstandings which students in the past experienced and which led to inappropriate lowering of academic expectations, and/or behavior management interventions, rather than a focus on challenging academics. In the fifties and early sixties, students who were not learning effectively were thought to be unable to learn because they were too limited in their general cognitive ability or because they were behaviorally or emotionally disturbed.

Leaders in the field of special education were perplexed about a group of students who had difficulty learning to read, write or do math; these students were failing to learn, but did not fit these two special education categories used at the time. They came to see that many of these students could understand complex, higher order ideas and were not necessarily behavior problems. Their problem was that they were hampered by disabilities in lower order information processing required to learn their basic skills. For example, many of these students had specific perceptual problems, such as difficulty distinguishing and manipulating sounds in spoken language, and with sounds and letters in reading and spelling. Some had lower memory difficulties, such as memory for factual information not integrated into meaningful concepts, e.g., the fifty states and capitals or the multiplication facts (Kauffman & Hallahan, 1981).

### The Overemphasis on Weaknesses

In the early grades, the basic skills are heavily dependent on the very areas which are problematic for many students with LD, and this results in an overemphasis on students' weaknesses (Gregg & Ferri, 1998). Notably, the much celebrated milestone of childhood—learning to read—is typically hindered, as is spelling and often writing. To feel unnerved or discouraged about not being able to meet parents' and teachers' expectations, and not being like one's peers, is a developmentally appropriate response. It is difficult to avoid the normal reaction of children to lose confidence in themselves as learners as they watch other children accomplishing these highly valued skills with relative ease.

Hence, it evolved that students with good academic potential who processed particular kinds of information differently for learning were categorized as students with learning disabilities. This clarified perspective and the term *learning disabilities* prevented misunderstanding and unnecessary hurt. As she reviewed her cases with this new perspective, one psychiatrist with whom I worked in these early years commented that she felt that she should write letters of apology to a number of these children she treated for years for "refusal to learn."

## Self-Knowledge from Diagnostic Testing

Information Meetings

Too often, due to the heavy case load, too much of the school psychologist's time is spent on evaluations to determine diagnostic labels rather than working with teachers and students on ways to improve student achievement. As a result, the reports have 'little instructional relevance' (OSEP, 1995, p. 10). It is important to have follow-up meetings with the psychologist for the explicit goal of gaining an in-depth, personal understanding of how the test performance informs the student's learning. The key is to make the evaluations 'instructionally relevant.'

If the psychologist is not available for meetings, it would be important to find another psychologist or an educational advocate to assist with interpretation of the diagnostic report. Educational advocates may be independent agents or volunteer advocates from agencies, such the state departments of education or teacher federations for students with special needs. For a percentage of their cases where needed, professional advocates specializing in learning disabilities may provide services without charge or on a sliding scale.

Gaining an In-depth Understanding

If it is possible to choose the tester, it is of value to have a licensed psychologist with a broad testing perspective do the diagnostic testing. To be useful, the psychologist's report should include, as well as grade or percentile levels in subject areas, the student's specific skill strengths and skill needs in relation to reading, writing and math. Additionally, a psychologist with an information processing or neuropsychological perspective can also provide relationships between the student's processing abilities—memory, attention, perception, conceptualization etc.—and the student's academic skills.

S/he can provide insights and explain the ways in which these abilities interact with the student's ability to form concepts and solve problems. Parents and students can ask the tester (and continue to ask themselves over time) such questions as: what are the student's difficulties with language, memory, attention, perception, spatial relations etc.; how do they interact with specific academic struggles; what are the student's strengths in comprehension, visual spatial, language, conceptual abilities etc.; how can the student strategize to use strengths to bypass academic difficulties and accomplish tasks through alternative routes?

Applying the Understanding Over Time

Relating the information to the various subject matter learning is not simple and is not accomplished in a few meetings; it is an on-going, long-term process. It is necessary, therefore, that a tutor, mentor or parent—some support person—participate in the follow-up meetings and acquire a solid grasp of the student's learning in order to assist the student over time in building the necessary body of strategies.  Adolescents naturally are concerned about the issue of independence and the suggestions for involving so many adults in their lives.  However, for students with LD, seeking out mentors and reaching out to family are behaviors associated with academic success and ultimately with independence (Hamilton & Hamilton, 1992; Hoy & Manglitz, 1996).

*Diagnostic Information for Documentation and Accommodations*

It is also of value to know that this type of specific diagnostic information is required as documentation for accommodation requests.  The identified ways in which the student's disabilities hinder test performance is required, for example, for extended time on standardized college entrance exams, SAT or ACT (See Appendix A for SAT and ACT accommodations).  Importantly, such diagnostic information continues to be needed for self-identification for eligibility of services and for academic accommodations requests in college (See Appendix B  for General Accommodations).

*Accentuating Strengths: Meeting College Admissions Requirements*

College Course Requirements

After gaining greater self-understanding, the next stage for students is to accentuate their intellectual strengths.  As they move up through the grades, students with LD express satisfaction that they find they are better able to experience and use their intellectual strengths.  Their understanding of challenging ideas in the content becomes more of an advantage than with the curriculum in earlier grades (Riley, 1998).  Students with LD who want to go to college should maintain high expectations and keep themselves in the college preparatory courses (See Appendix A for college course requirements, timing, sequence and questions to ask your college counselor).

Balancing the Courseload

It is of great value to take care to balance the courseload carried each year—a balance between the courses the student finds most difficult with courses in the student's areas of strength.  If this isn't workable, to relieve pressure during the school year, it may even be wise to take some of the most challenging courses in the summer, one at a time, at a nearby accredited preparatory school or community college.  The intense, singular focus can facilitate the grasp of the material.  Permission to get credit for summer school courses usually requires approval by the high school administration.

Identifying Content Area Strengths

For the student's self esteem and academic record, focusing on a strength area and achieving in a challenging academic subject area clearly demonstrates the students' intellectual capability, to themselves and others.  Students work out which subject areas fit their strong points and build those areas to the level where they excel—and can enjoy the academic accomplishment.  Selecting a subject area takes careful consideration because, surprisingly, different cognitive strengths are called upon even in closely related academic areas.  In science, for example, if chemistry proves to be very difficult for a student, biology very well could turn out to be a strength area.  Even those students with LD who have difficulties with expository writing—where they strain to convey factual knowledge in an organized fashion in reports—may find that they have talents for creative writing, for fiction or poetry (Riley, 1999a).

*Standardized Test Requirements and Strengths*

As well as the regularly required SAT I Math and English tests, many colleges additionally require three, subject-specific SAT II Achievement Tests. Students should plan to make the content areas in which they are building depth be the ones they will eventually take in the SAT II Achievement Tests or for the (voluntary) Advanced Placement Tests AP (See Appendix A). Students benefit from taking the SAT II tests close in time to taking the content area courses related to that achievement test. Local colleges offer summer school courses which students could take—not necessarily for grades or credit—but rather to deepen their knowledge further in the specific content area, perhaps the summer before they plan to take a particular SAT II test. Some students choose to take the summer course before they take the high school course.

Students may repeat the SAT I content areas of Math and English as one or two of the subjects for their SAT II subject-specific Achievement tests. If they do not want to do their achievement tests in either Math or English, they need to plan to gain depth in three other content areas for the SAT II Achievement tests. It is also worth checking whether the colleges where one is thinking of applying require that students take SAT IIs in particular content areas. Locale of the college relates to whether the SAT or ACT is required (See Appendix A). Many students find it advantageous to take the SATs more than once to improve scores.

## Part II 'Know How' for Coping in the General Education Classroom

*Understanding the Environmental Realities to Understand Oneself*

To develop a well-grounded self-knowledge a student needs to be able to distinguish when the factors creating challenges are internal to oneself or external, environmental factors—or both. To resolve the issue, one has to know what needs to be modified and where and how to place precious time and energy. It is a healthy stance for the student to ask, first, *"What do I need to do? What have I not done? How could I find a way to compensate and fit into the general education system?"* It is, of course, important not to place the responsibility on external causes without thinking the situation through. However, one of the issues which students need to understand is that sometimes there are factors in their academic setting that reasonably need to be altered (See Appendix B Accommodations).

The 'Try Harder' Mandate

Due to hard, even painful struggles with learning, students with LD have a particular need to experience the relationship between effort and achievement (Vaidya, 1999). In order to develop trust in their own abilities, students need to know when it is their efforts or capabilities that are the issue and when it is not. Students with LD often express that they have had doubts about their abilities from having been told so often, "If you would just 'try harder.'" As one student said in a very difficult context, "I'm trying harder, and I'm doing worse. And then I wonder if it's worth it to keep trying." It is crucial for academic achievement for students to understand what went right as well as what went wrong—and why—in order to gain control over the academic outcomes of their efforts (Hagborg, 1999). The relationship between experiencing control over one's environment and enhanced motivation has long been established (Dweck, & Leggett, 1988; Zimmerman, 2000).

Full-time Inclusion Still Needs Improvement

Students need to know, therefore, that leaders in the field of special education have stated—and have demonstrated by research in the classroom—that the necessary changes in general education required to support the academic needs of students with learning disabilities in full-time inclusion have not yet been accomplished (Baker & Zigmond, 1995; Lenz, et al., 1995; Zigmond, Jenkins, Fuchs, et al., 1995). Students planning to go to college must be in the general education inclusionary or mainstream classes, and it is particularly challenging for professionals to design inclusionary curriculum to support both students who are college bound, as well as those who are not (Edgar & Polloway, 1994).

This is not a criticism of the teachers; teachers themselves express that they feel frustrated that, under the present conditions, they cannot do what they know needs to be done, such as make instructional adaptations or find time to collaborate with special educators (Morocco, Riley, & Gordon, 1995; Riley & Morocco, 1999). At the secondary level, the collaboration model among professionals is especially challenging; the greater numbers of students, staff and departments in high schools result in a complex interaction of people and programs (Ellett, 1993).

Seeking Reasonable Accommodations and Support

The United States is one of the few nations in the world attempting the idealistic goal of mass education. We are still in the process of learning how to educate all of our students, especially those who learn differently. To cope with some conditions, therefore, it is an intelligent and appropriate strategy for students to seek additional support or to request a reasonable accommodation—and not to interpret all obstacles as possible to overcome on their own (See Appendix B & Appendix C).

*What the Students Have to Say about High School*

Surveys of Student Opinions

In studies surveying the opinions of high school students with learning disabilities, the students express that, layered on top of the usual high school pressures that exist for all college bound students, they do experience additional academic frustration (Guterman, 1995; Kotering & Braziel, 1999b; Seidal & Vaughn, 1991). Their feelings of frustration increase as they move from elementary to Junior High or Middle School, and frustration escalates markedly with the programming models at the High School level (Eccles & Midgley, 1990; Ellett, 1993). Students with LD from high-income backgrounds have been found to be somewhat more positive about their educational opportunities than others (Vaughn & Klinger, 1998). This may relate to more extensive individualized support available in advantaged families, availability of adult time for mentoring and the financial means to provide out-of-school academic supports and enrichment.

Drop-out Rates and Grades

Generally, however, student expression of stress is consistent with the studies that show that drop-out rates for high school students with LD is double the rate of students in the general population (Capital Publications, 1997; Kortering & Braziel, 1999b; Whinnery, 1993). Consistent also is that national surveys report that high school students with LD mainstreamed in the general education programs, in spite of average or above intelligence, have lower grade point averages than their non-LD peers (Bursuck, Munk & Olson, 1999; Bursuck, Polloway, Plante, et al., 1996). A consistent finding is that students hold their special education teachers personally in high regard, but strongly voice the need for more individualized instructional time and mentoring by all of their teachers and by administrators (Hamilton & Hamilton, 1992; Vaughn & Klinger, 1998). Students with learning disabilities doing well need to appreciate themselves for their hard earned success.

### *The Realities and Hurdles from the Teachers' Perspective*
Coordinating General and Special Education Systems

Knowing the realities and limitations of the environment saves a student wasted time and energy over presently unalterable conditions. One of the major differences in special education programming at the high school level is that there is not a parallel curriculum between general and special education (Ellett, 1993). In earlier grades, the basic skills are addressed in the curriculum of both systems, reading skills, writing book reports, math fundamentals etc. In high school, the interface for curriculum is more problematic.

> Expecting secondary special education teachers to teach all basic and content area courses, even in areas where they are unendorsed, was the supervisors' of high school special education second most often expressed practice that should be discontinued (Houck , Engelhard, & Geller, 1990, p. 322).

Secondary LD teachers express the concern about their ability to provide sufficient instructional time for their students scheduled for special services (Houck et al., 1990). As well as the breadth of the content in the varied subjects that students bring to LD specialists for content clarification and test preparation, the specialists are also responsible for determining how much remediation of weak basic skills should continue to be the focus of high school special education support. Time is spent on basic skills, but with some students reporting that the instruction is on lower level skills that are simply repetitive for them (Houck, et al., 1990; Guterman, 1995). The issue of where to focus available instruction time is debated: do minimal changes in basic skills at this stage justify the time and energy spent (Whinnery, 1992)? Since time is so limited, one argument is that time needs to be selectively used only for basic skills that are clearly receptive to change (Houck, 1990).
Amount of Content and Numbers of Students

General education teachers in high school inclusionary classes report that they are increasingly under pressure to "cover the content." Their teaching is affected by the demands for increased curriculum content prescribed by the local school system, state standards, and the college entrance achievement examinations; this results in a hurried pace in their instruction (Lenz, et al., 1995). As well, it is not unusual for high school teachers to be responsible for five periods per day of classes, with twenty to twenty-five students per class—one hundred to one hundred and twenty-five students per day. Additionally, classes include a wide range of instructional needs due to the increasingly diverse population of students with English as a second language, as well as the inclusion of students with special learning needs (Boudah, Deshler & Schumaker, 1997).

Whole Class Instruction

These factors force a whole-class instructional model with little or no time to stop for individualized teacher-student interactions (Hagborg, 1999; Lenz et al., 1995; Schumm et al., 1995). Direct observation of classes finds few examples of instructional modification for clarification or explanation (Baker & Zigmond, 1995; McIntosh, Vaughn, Schumm, Haager & Lee, 1994). Yet, the importance of individual student feedback has been identified as one of the critical elements in instruction for effective inclusion (Lenz, et al., 1995; Morocco, Riley, & Gordon, 1995; Schumaker & Deshler, 1988).

The conclusion reached by some high school teachers is that high school must be a place where students learn to make it on their own or to seek out ways to get the help they need (Schumm et al., 1995). It appears paradoxical to talk about independence and seeking support as companions, but they are two sides of the same coin. It is by making use of the necessary additional instructional support services—mentors, tutors, parents—that students with LD learn to develop the strategies, adaptations and accommodations they need to reach the independence they want and require for college.

**Part III  Becoming Strategic: Building the Repertoire of Personal Strategies**

*Defining Strategy*

Stated most simply, a strategy is finding "a way to go" to solve a problem or to reach a goal. It is a procedure or a method with an orderly set of steps or it can be likened to a "mini system." Becoming strategic requires—knowing that there are different kinds of knowing. A strategy involves *knowing how* to go about accomplishing a task or solving a problem. It also presupposes that one will be calling up from memory basic information. That is, *knowing that*: students need to *know that* the steps in the procedure include the particular set of actions. They also may *know that*, for example, a problem is a time-distance problem. They then need to *know how* to go about solving it— search out, figure out—what is the appropriate strategy to apply. Increasing aware-ness of these subtle distinctions in thinking and knowing requires deliberate instruction.

> A legitimate and preeminent principle of educating a student with a
> learning disability is based on the assumption that 'teaching that' and
> 'teaching how' must precede 'knowing that' and 'knowing how'
> (Simmons & Kameenui, 1988, p. 394).

*The Need for Strategy Instruction*

Without the benefit of instruction and guidance, it has been found that many students with LD tend not to, spontaneously, employ this search for the needed strategy in an ambiguous situation (Swanson, 1990). Students with LD have the ability to strategize, but it is as if their computer doesn't default into a strategizing mode to get started.

Another tendency is that the students with LD are inclined to stick with familiar strategies, even when they are not particularly effective (Torgensen, 1980). Yet, importantly, research has demonstrated that, with instruction, students with LD have learned and generalized strategies in ways that have enabled them to master complex academic work (Boudah et al., 1997).

Another common reaction, however, for many students with LD to strategy instruction is to be anxious to 'get the work done' and not to take the time to stop to reflect on the process of building strategies. They need to be made aware of the worth of the strategies as they are learning them. If students evaluate, select, and adjust the strategies, the numbers of strategies get narrowed down, become habituated, and the effortfulness is markedly reduced. Initially, in order to gain the motivation to persist, students need mentoring or tutorial support to help them reflect upon their own processing. That is, to experience and note the efficiency of the strategy and to see the connection between the successful outcomes and the strategy (Hoffman & Field, 1995).

### Metacognition: Paying Attention to One's Own Thinking

The term "cognition" refers to thinking and knowing. "Meta" here means "above" or "transcending." Metacognition can be thought of as rising above —climbing up above oneself —and looking down upon one's own thoughts. Metacognition is the technical term for *thinking about one's own thinking and knowing about one's own knowing*. It also includes *knowing when one knows and knowing when does not know*. For students with LD, metacognition has been found to be one of the most powerful tools to gain control over their problem areas in processing information and to increase achievement (Pressley, Harris & Guthrie, 1992).

The combination of *self-knowledge* and *metacognition* can help to demystify the sources of confusion and frustration which have been a part of many students' learning throughout their schooling.

### Talking to Yourself

Talking to oneself may be commonly associated with behavior that is sometimes thought of as strange. For those who don't tend to talk to themselves very much, however, it is actually an important skill they need to develop. Effective problem solvers talk to themselves. It provides the opportunity to reflect— to stop and take the time for a second look at what is being asked—and provides the chance to clarify the situation. It allows for a better response, especially for a complicated task. Students may feel pressure from others to give a response before they are ready. Many students also experience their own urge to respond too quickly—perhaps to 'get it over with.' One cognitive intervention program provides the students with a phrase to say to themselves (or to others) when they feel that pressure to respond too quickly —'Just a minute, let me think' (Elliott, 1993).

Talking aloud is a form of "thinking aloud." Voicing one's own thinking and hearing that thinking can strengthen metacognition.

**Maureen K. Riley, M.Ed.**

**Self-questioning**

The self-questioning is another form of the students' talking to themselves, being reflective and metacognitive.

*What is causing me the most difficulty with this assignment? What is it that I do—or don't do—in my reading that makes it difficult? What is it about writing papers that I don't get them done on time? On what parts do I get stuck? Which kinds of papers are the hardest for me? In what kinds of work do I feel the most frustration? What subjects are the easiest for me? the most difficult? Where do I do best in math? Algebra? Geometry? Where do I get confused in math? With which kinds of problems?...with basic facts?...with recognizing what kind of problem it is? Is it a problem with finding the right procedures to solve the problem or remembering the steps of the procedure? What gets in the way of my realizing when assignments are due?*

The important next set of questions which can lead directly to active strategizing: *What could I do about...(any and all of the above)?*

***Strengthening Strategies through Dialogue***

Some students are able to talk about strategies but, even then, do not apply them (O'Neill and Douglas, 1991). Working on assignments with a mentor one-on-one, or in a small group, provides the time and opportunity for *dialogue*, for exchange of ideas.

Engaging in dialogue provides a structure for students to practice the strategy of going back over their thinking and expressing aloud the reasoning that led them to the place where they were stopped. Even simple verification from another that the student's thinking is 'on mark' is important for the consolidation and progress of the student's learning. Students with LD tend not to go back over and recheck their work on their own (Meltzer, Roditi, Houser & Perlman, 1998). There is something about having to explain to another person that presents a demand and keeps one on target. The mentor can *mediate* their learning, that is, not 'tell' but —assess the student's cognitive efforts where steps are missing or misapplied; pose probing questions to stimulate student insight around those places; if needed, model partial approaches (Riley & Morocco, 1999).

Students rethink and fill in on their own or can explain back what has been modeled. They reason through the set of facts —looking for and pointing up the relationships across the information, expressing the connections between steps —not just repeating or verbalizing. Explaining aloud provides the opportunity to see the sources of their confusion or to reflect upon the connections to gain insight into how their thinking moved forward. It is not uncommon for students to begin quickly to clarify their own thinking, 'Oh, I see, this is where I went off...this is what I need to do.' They are enabled to construct their own meaning because they are not simply 'told.' They are enabled to climb up and reach the goal on their own because they have been provided the necessary scaffolding in the mentoring process (Wood, Bruner & Ross, 1976).

***Personalizing Strategies***

What is known is that strategies need to be personalized; students need to find the strategies that fit them individually and that work with their strengths and compensate for their personal need areas (Borkowski & Muthukrishna, 1992). Individualization is necessary because the category, learning disabilities, encompasses such a heterogeneous group of students that, therefore, there are not generic strategies that will work for all students (Swanson et al., 1996). Students frequently say, "That just doesn't work for me." For example, one student may need to "ball park" very quickly what the answer to a problem may be in order to get started. That strategy is anathema to some students; to get a sense of what is needed, they need to clarify the parts of the problem, piece by piece, and only then stand back and look at it as a whole.

Different strategies need to be tried out and then continued to be honed to fit the individual student and to become increasingly efficient. After ball-parking, some students need to find a 'next' strategy to be able to begin to work the problem. They may have to be encouraged to use the strategy of talking through with a partner what cues or reasons were used as a basis for the estimate or 'guess.' Strategies are best developed during the process of students doing their real class assignments and with students reflecting on what personally makes sense to them. They discuss which strategies, and how the strategies, have made a difference for them in that context. They also benefit from thinking about how the strategies could be useful with other settings and tasks (Montague, 1993; Swanson et al., 1996).

## Part IV  Applying the Strategizing to the Schoolwork
### *Self-monitoring and Planning: Overseeing and Managing Strategies*

Effective strategizing is guided by continual *self-monitoring and planning*. Both self-monitoring and planning have been identified as particular areas of need for students with LD (Wong, Wong, Blenkinsop, 1989). The term *executive functioning* is one of the significant but still fuzzy concepts. However, it is very helpful as an image. It helps to sum up the need for this issue of the overall managing of one's thinking. Like the chief executive officer of a business, students need to be in control of the various departments of their thinking and working: recalling what they know about a problem; holding onto to that information while deciding what is new; predicting what else will be needed; splicing the new ideas with what they already know; selecting and recalling the procedures needed; applying the procedures; testing out the solution, etc. They need to be overseeing, planning, and juggling these different kinds of ideas and actions that are happening to "get the job done" and come up with the product or the solution.

Another term that helps to illustrate these behaviors is called *self-regulation*. Students who are self-regulated are self-aware learners, setting goals or plans; evaluating how well or poorly they are performing; understanding that success is related to effort and persistence; and knowing when to seek help (Zimmerman, 2000).

### *Adolescent Thinking and the Ability to Oversee Strategies*

As they reach adolescence, it is important for students with LD to know that they are at a significantly higher cognitive level developmentally. Their cognitive abilities have developed to a new, adult stage of thinking referred to as the capacity for 'formal thought.' It is a time to try new ways of approaching learning, gaining control, and experiencing the efficacy of and satisfaction from learning. Students with LD, especially, need to learn to make use of these higher order capabilities in their academic work

(Guterman, 1995). Years of remedial subskill instruction can be so dominant for students with LD that a great deal of time and energy has been drained away from experiencing the satisfaction of their higher order abilities.

Adolescents have cognitive capabilities well beyond those of younger children. They now have greater control over earlier pitfalls, such as getting stuck on singular factors that can be compelling and dominating, or being generally overwhelmed by complexity. They have gained the ability to manipulate broad concepts and to think about them in a systematic way. As adolescents, they are now able to see the large picture; juggle the factors; rule out the extraneous and the trivial; consider other possible additions or hypotheses to work toward the solution of a problem.

It is true that some of the very difficulties associated with LD can get in the way of higher order thinking. However, adolescents now can begin to identify the specific sources of their quandary, and this is their opening to gain greater control. For example, if their diagnostic testing shows that the students' tendency is to become over-focused and miss the big picture, they are able to guide themselves to step back and to self-question. In reading comprehension, they can self-question: *what is this all about; what does the author think is so important that he is bothering to tell about this; what would he argue for; what do all these pieces add up to; what big point is being made?* Some students become under-focused and get the gist of things, but miss the important details. They can self-monitor and direct themselves to go back through and ask themselves which specifics inform, shape, make a difference to the big ideas, and then select and circle those specifics.

### *Task Analysis and Getting Started with Assignments*

Formal thought allows students to take a task apart, to use an important and useful coping mechanism. That is, *task analysis*. Task analysis involves taking a "meta" view of a job to be done—looking down on it as an entity to see what it entails. A task, of course, can be any piece of work, any class assignment—an essay to write, a math problem to solve, a report or project to complete. So that they don't have to hold it all in their heads, some students take out the "pieces" or sections of the problem and draw a kind of a flow chart or map; some prefer to write out a list of the parts or subsets.

### Where to Begin

An issue for many students with LD is that the parts of the assignment do not appear obvious—do not "stand out" for them. If the structure or framework isn't evident, deciding how to begin—where to pick up a piece to begin to work —becomes a problem. Unfortunately, this situation can be interpreted as procrastination, avoidance due to laziness, stubbornness etc. Students' confidence in themselves can be diminished. One student commented:

> I began to ask myself if maybe I am just lazy—cause I just find lots of ways to get up and get away from it—or maybe I'm stupid cause I know I really do want to do it—but I just sit there so long and don't really do anything.

### Finding the Blueprint

Students need to see the construction of assignments; they need to be able to become aware that they there is a kind of "blueprint" of the job. This is another area where many students legitimately require support in order to become independent. They often don't have awareness of what it is that is stopping them. A person who is an expert on problem solving today reflects on his experience with this type of frustration as a student and encourages the intervention of mentors:

> I was enormously irritated by the hundreds of hours that I wasted staring at problems without any good idea about what approach to try next in attempting to solve them. I thought at the time that there was no educational value in those 'blank' minutes, and I see no value in them today (Wickelgren, 1974, p. ix).

Tacit Knowledge

The adults supporting the students may not be able to see the source of students' difficulty with task analysis because the structure and parts (or steps) are so obvious to them. Adults can have a *tacit* knowledge of activities, particularly with tasks they do very automatically. Tacit is a subtle concept; it refers to "things unspoken" or unexplained. It can be that adults themselves know how to do, but they don't necessarily have an explicit, organized formulation of the steps of the task in their own thinking which they can easily share. Parents or tutors can work on task analysis with students by asking together: *Just what is involved here; what are the steps needed to get this done?* Adults need to be sure to include all of the steps, even those that may appear, to them, too obvious or minor to list.

### *Task Analysis with Writing and Reading Tasks*

To complete classroom assignments, research has shown that students' difficulties can be heightened by the problem of tacit knowledge. For example, in a federal reading-writing research study on inclusion working with effective, experienced teachers, it was found that even these capable teachers took for granted that all of their students understood what the writing of a personal narrative involved. It became obvious that the diverse needs in their inclusionary classroom required more explicit instruction for particular students, and particularly for the students with LD (Riley, Morocco & Gordon, 1993). Some students had equated the writing task with a description of a personal event, but one that did not fulfill the genre of personal narrative. The goal was to improve the written products by defining specifically what was lacking in the writing to empower the students to improve and to learn for the future—not simply to place a low grade on those papers. It turned out to be a challenging task to provide the specific guidance the students needed.

The Personal Narrative

Both teachers and researchers enjoyed having the luxury of time that the research study provided to reflect and to develop a clear, explicit understanding of all of the *components of personal narrative.* For example, they determined that the personal event selected also needed to involve...a restricted time frame...a brief, 'bracketed' episode or experience with a tension and resolution, a beginning, middle and end...nonfiction...of high value to the author that evokes mood...with vivid details which elicit feeling in the reader... (Riley et al., 1993, p. 195).

Taking this perspective was working at the "meta" level—that is, a meta-awareness—looking down upon the task from "above"—as something to be observed and analyzed to gain a better understanding of what it is all about.

This process clarified instruction and provided specific and individual guidance for students. Some students had chosen stories too long to tell, and after pages had not come near completing the narrative; it was not "bracketed." Others had chosen events that were not story-like, that is, descriptions of events without any problems or tension, without a beginning, middle and end. Some needed to create mood by providing specific images or by describing their own intense reactions. The framework elicited lively and substantive class discussion about tension, mood, examples of "imageable" details. Teachers judged that all of the students' final products benefited. More importantly, students increased their meta-awareness of the components of a personal narrative and were able to produce a better product with the next assignment.

Analyzing the Structure of Story

Other metacognitive frameworks address the problem of tacit knowledge and contribute to skill building in both reading and writing. For example, *story schema* can enhance reading comprehension of narratives or creating a narrative. If students can be brought to a heightened awareness there are predictable parts or components of most stories, their reading comprehension can be enhanced (Cain, 1996). Stories most often are made up of elements: the setting; a hero or main characters; a problem to be solved; attempts at solving that problem; failures or successful solution; and how the character(s) feels about the outcome (Rumelhart, 1980). Terms, such as 'setting' need to be discussed to include time (era), as well as place. Until familiarity of the story structure becomes automatic, students can be supported by use of a question/answer form which alerts them to the schema as they read. The questions name the elements and asks them to identify and make notes about the elements as they arise in the story (Riley, 1983).

*Transferring Strategies Across Subject Areas*

In-depth understanding includes genuine transfer. In other words, the students independently demonstrate the ability to apply their learned strategies and knowledge in a new context. The students approach with ways of figuring out the new problem. The most common strategy is to search out what is alike or different from what one already knows. A student who sees every new chemistry formula as a totally different entity—rather than seeking out the ways in which the formula is made up of familiar chunks or subsets—would be forced to brute memorize endlessly and would soon be overwhelmed.

*Activating Prior Knowledge: Bridging and Linking*

It is helpful for students to know that some strategies have been studied and found to be highly useful and transferable. There are sets of strategies applied *before, during* and *after* reading challenging text which can be applied to varied subject matter areas. Applied to text, as well as science formulas, the strategy that encourages students to "stir up," recall, (and with reading, often share in a group), whatever they might know about a topic *before* beginning to read is labeled *activating prior knowledge*. The process is also to referred to as *bridging* or *linking* what one already knows to what is new. Alerting oneself to "tie in" with new material what one already knows is a strategy for learning across the board.

### Prior Knowledge and Self-questioning and Predicting

Before beginning to read, the student takes note of the title and the bolded terms that introduce paragraphs (or within paragraphs), and seeks out definitions of unfamiliar terms. Less skilled comprehenders show less awareness of how helpful the title can be to provide information about the main themes. Pre-reading also includes skimming charts or pictures and possibly the first sentences of paragraphs. The students ask themselves: What do these terms, pictures and charts remind me of; what else do I already know about that? Talking with others at this stage is helpful. In a group or with a partner, sharing each others' thoughts can stimulate more associations or clarify ones that may be incompatible. "Waking up" what is already in a student's mind on the topic allows the reader to take the next pre-reading steps: to make guesses or predictions about what the text may be about. Students then create a few questions that the text might answer. If it is the kind of material that allows for visualizing, imaging also can aid with comprehension.

### Marking the Text to Self-Monitor and Activate Thinking

During reading, one of the most critical factors is to be monitoring whether one is relating to the text and comprehending. Self monitoring is a skill that needs to be strengthened for many students with LD. It is not unusual to hear the comments, such as, "When I've read through the whole thing, I don't know what I read, and I have to read it all over again;" or "I understood it as I read it, but can't remember what I read afterwards." Marking the text every few lines in various ways can ensure engagement with the text:

- stars beside a line that seems important
- question marks where the text is confusing or just not understood
- a word or two—yes! for something of interest or agreement, no! for disagreement with the idea of the author
- a couple of words for a related idea that comes to mind
- a happy face (or mad) face where one can get a strong emotional response
- minimally represent a visual image in some way, if possible.

The varied purposes of the marks encourage different types of active learning. Requiring oneself to make marks on a regular basis can serve to habituate engagement with the text. When a question mark comes up, it can be used as a signal to reread just those couple of lines. If the confusion is clarified, an "OK" can go next to the question mark. If rereading a sentence or two doesn't help, seek out definitions of terms or add another question mark as a reminder to seek out further information or clarification from another.

The kinds of marks made can indicate how much is being gained from the text. Too many question marks may mean more intensive pre-reading is needed, or it may even indicate that more background knowledge is required before that text can be read and comprehended. Ideal is that the students own a copy of their textbooks so they are free to write in them. If not possible, pages can be Xeroxed to practice the marking process.

### Summarizing in Phrases

Another highly valuable, but challenging strategy is to force oneself to summarize a paragraph by writing only a couple of phrases in the margin using one's own words. Self-questioning comes in: What if I were limited to only a couple of three-word phrases, what could I write? Initially, many students find this a difficult process, but they become appreciative of the results. At first, it is helpful to have a partner scribe the phrases, and then the two work together to shorten the language by deleting any non-essential words. Using one's own words is a key factor, not words from the text. The process of sifting back through the paragraph—judging what is more or less essential—what could be left out, of course, is the difficult part. It takes time and practice and, for many students, initially requires guidance and discussion. However, while one is making these judgments about the material, learning of the content is taking place; the time spent poring over the material actually becomes useful study time.

If the selection is not too long, to apply the process for each paragraph, or two at a time, is much easier than for several paragraphs or for the entire selection. The phrases provide efficient review because they are brief and personal, and therefore meaningful. They also provide the students with ready language to answer questions about the text. Note taking, in general, also needs to follow these guidelines to be effective. It must be highly selective and thoughtfully paraphrased, not simply a literal "lifting out" of the author's words.

### Dialoguing with a Reading Partner

After reading, satisfying and effective is to explain what one has read to another, to discuss the ideas and together to formulate a summary. Some students find sharing and summarizing by mapping out the ideas in some graphic form helpful. There are variations on a reading strategy referred to as partner reading or pair reading. One reads a paragraph aloud, then both discuss; then the roles switch. To comprehend while reading aloud is difficult for some students as is listening to oral reading. If that is the case, one or both can read the same paragraph silently and then discuss. Sharing the meaning of the paragraph can be particularly effective in a tutorial when one partner has broader knowledge on the topic and/or has strong reading skills to model. To observe how another person associates to the text to make meaning can be very valuable for some students with comprehension difficulties.

### Meta-View of the Purpose for Reading

Taking a meta-view of the purpose for which one is reading can also serve to focus the reader's thinking in different ways and can guide the student in how to vary strategies. Reading a chapter for homework as preparation for class in contrast to reading to prepare for a test the next day, calls for a different level of demand for memory of detail. Tests vary, preparing for a history test with fill-in-the-blanks requires recall of the information whereas multiple choice items call for recognition memory. Reading for an English essay test which will ask for a personal response to a piece of literature differs again. It is a fair question to ask the teacher what kind of response mode will be required, as well as when the tests will be. Anticipating the timing and the kinds of tests and keeping up with homework assignments are two basics which reduce failure and prevent students from experiencing a lack of control. Initially, students with LD genuinely need parental or tutorial support to learn to handle this type of communication with teachers about types of tests, as well as generally with due dates and overall management of time.

## *Meta-Memory and Strategizing*

Establishing Meaningfulness

Being aware of the different kinds of memory required for tests leads into the category of meta-memory— again, the process is a subset of metacognition—looking down upon the category of memory and becoming more aware of different kinds of memory. Students need to become strategic and be aware of the choices of ways to memorize for different tasks. Many students with LD also need to be particularly cognizant of the memory issue mentioned above: that students with LD typically have difficulty holding onto material that is not meaningful to them. Without meaning, they are then left in the position to learn by rote. This is one of the main reasons why it is critical for students to take the initiative and seek out clarification of work they have not fully grasped; the meaningfulness and understanding strengthen memory. Yet, it has been found that students with LD rarely ask for help from teachers or peers (McIntosh et al., 1994).

This is where students with LD can intentionally make use of their good conceptual abilities. When there is a solid, meaningful grasp of a concept or an idea, the related information gets "tied in." Meaningfulness is when the student persists to the place that s/he personally sees how the parts make sense —how and why they fit together. In turn, this is what holds the information together and stores it as an integrated concept in memory. When it is tied-in within an organized whole, it can be retrieved more easily. Seeking out assistance for understanding is worth the effort also because rote memory of material is typically boring, difficult—and is not lasting.

Using Mnemonics

The environmental realities enter again and do have to be considered. It has been found that in high school a high percentage of quizzes and exams are made up of questions requiring a heavy load of factual information which is not easily meaningfully integrated. Also, these tests determine a significant proportion of report card grades (Putnam, 1992a). Students, therefore, need instruction in memory techniques to deal with factual recall, with items, such as Eli Whitney invented the cotton gin. In such cases, mnemonics can be applied.

Mnemonics are memory aids, techniques used to associate factual information—but in ways that are rather artificial. That is, the facts are interrelated, but usually in far-fetched, maybe even peculiar or humorous ways. The students find a relationship between the facts to be linked and associate them with something else that is well established in their own memories. For example, it may be a very familiar word, such as HOMES, which can serve as an acronym, that is, a word where each letter of the word is the first letter of the set of facts to remember. HOMES is a common mnemonic acronym for recalling the first letters of the names of the five Great Lakes: Huron, Ontario, Michigan, Erie and Superior. Making memories concrete is another mnemonic technique. Students might add a visual component, such as picturing homes at the edge of a lake to lock in the word to be remembered. With detailed verbal information, letter patterns can be used. To remember whether to use "there" or "their" in a sentence, students might remember that the word "here" is inside the word "there" and both can refer to a place. Some students develop long and cumbersome connections, e.g., "their" is the possessive and "hers" and "his" are possessive and have "e" and "i" in the middle—and girls before boys, so "ei." As strange and cumbersome one's own associations appear to others, they can function well for that person because they are personal.

Some find that humor helps. An Algebra teacher created a mnemonic for a strategy with the acronym SSAD: $\underline{S}$ame sign, $\underline{S}$ubtract, $\underline{A}$dd for $\underline{D}$ifferent signs.

> Remembering that simultaneous equations are 'SSAD' at least gives students the chance to laugh at one of the very taxing aspects of math with which they have to cope (MacDonald, 1999, p. 13).

There are many other techniques that combine phonetic, sound-alike cues and visual cues related to the factual information. A college student had difficulty remembering what the word 'ramifications' meant in an exam question asking about the ramifications of certain environmental hazards. So for the future, he thought of the animal, ram, and then pictured the ram battering a wall and the wall breaking up to associate the definition, 'consequences.' These and other strategies have been demonstrated to be helpful to students with LD for the critical goal of survival in the commonly used, fact-based tests (Bulgren, Schumaker, & Deshler, 1994; Mastropieri & Scruggs, 1998; Scruggs & Mastropieri, 1993).

Limits of Mnemonics

Mnemonics can be valuable also to store procedural information needed frequently in problem solving, such as with SSAD, and the frequent use can help to maintain the cue. However, there are clear limits to mnemonic techniques, and they are not presented here as a preferred way of learning. Piling up large numbers of mnemonics can become confusing. For material that is very heavily loaded with factual information, mnemonics have been shown to be less successful (Stephens & Dwyer, 1997). Much of the information stored with mnemonics is not well maintained over time (Thomas & Wang, 1996). Mnemonics, then, should be used wisely, only when there is not a meaningful alternative. Students report also that, though rote memory and mnemonics were helpful in high school, they were less useful in college. Exams in college more frequently involve problem solving which requires conceptual understanding and integration of information (Riley, 1998).

Superficial Strategies

Students benefit from understanding the distinction between superficial strategies for short term value versus strategies that lead to integrated conceptual learning that facilitate storage in long term memory. For example, verbal rehearsal, repeating information over and over, may serve to hold onto a phone number for a short time, but has been shown to be ineffective for maintaining information long term (Thomas & Wang, 1996). Simply highlighting most of what is on a page of text as a strategy indicates that the student isn't calling attention to what is most important to foster comprehension or to heighten what is to be remembered. Staying on the surface of the text, using reading and rereading as a strategy—waiting for the eventual "sink in" to take place—is time consuming and discouraging. To foster comprehension and enhance memory students need to "actively engage" with the material, such as in the varied ways modeled above in "marking the text."

### Strategy Program Recognizing Student Needs

The laws direct that students with disabilities be planful and proactive, be involved in their transition planning and in the long term planning of their future. Concretely, it is stated that students have the opportunity to be involved in the development of their IEPs and, importantly, in the evaluation of the outcomes of their IEPs (IDEA, 1990).

IEPs are mandated to identify the needs of the student and what the services will be to support those needs; to anticipate what the outcomes of this planning should be; and then to evaluate the outcomes (Federal Register, 1981). Many secondary school students, however, do not participate in creating or evaluating the effectiveness of their programs (Durlak, 1994; Houck, 1990).

For students with LD to participate meaningfully and follow this mandate, they need the in-depth understanding of their learning strengths and needs described above to be able to select and develop appropriate adaptations and accommodations. Students do need mentoring—that is guidance, coaching, tutoring—to learn how to participate effectively in these meetings (See Appendix D).

There are programs designed to address these needs. For example, IPLAN is an acronym to address the necessary elements for student participation in long term planning and for communication; the skills needed at IEP meetings. The acronym stands for: Inventorying of self knowledge; Providing the information from the self-inventory; Listening; Asking questions; and Naming goals (Van Reusen & Bos, 1990).

The IPLAN program acknowledges that for students to accomplish these skills requires intensive support. The program includes training with professionals in small student groups, daily, for forty-five minutes, for one to two weeks. The first, highly complex step, Inventorying, involves adult support for the students to reflect upon, identify and record their strengths and needs. The adults ask guiding questions—as broad as topics of career goals, social and academic strengths and needs. They also ask the student questions as specific as the kinds of materials, activities, and group size that are personally beneficial for that student's learning, and the kinds of test questions with which the student is most successful.

The last four steps deal with the communication skills. The adults model the skills and support the students as they practice the skills. As follow-up the students continue with the tasks. Over time, the students monitor, update, and report their progress in these areas and present the update to the professionals involved. Of course, the ability to answer these topics doesn't happen overnight. It is a long term process continuing into college, but it does become easier over time. The elements of the IPLAN program reflect many of the elements of the strategic mindset and the program states clearly the need for professional support.

## Part V   Looking Forward to College

*Progress in the Development of Support Systems and Accommodations*

In spite of the challenges along the way, students with learning disabilities can now realistically look forward to attending and enjoying college. Tens of thousands of students with learning disabilities have been attending college since the 1980s (Shapiro & Rich, 1999). These students have established a groundwork that makes life better for students with LD arriving on college campuses today. The principles of the Americans with Disabilities Act (ADA) have been applied and tested at the college level (Gordon, & Keiser, 1998). Critically supportive accommodations, such as extended time for examinations, tape recorded textbooks etc. have been judged to be necessary and reasonable for students with documented learning disabilities, and importantly, have been judged to be the responsibility of the colleges to grant them to students whose documentation supports the need (Guckenberger v. Boston University). (See Appendix B).

*Factors Associated with Success in College*

Many college students with learning disabilities report that, the reality is, that they do have to work very hard, but that they are succeeding and enjoying their college experience (Riley, 1998; Vogel & Adelman, 1993). Successful students with LD report that one of the important ways they have coped is by taking great care to select a college with strong support services. Making use of those support services then has allowed them to continue to grow in understanding themselves in the college context. This understanding increases their ability to self-advocate with faculty and administration for reasonable accommodations. The academic support helps both the rate and quality of the production of the school work—getting it done—getting it done well—and getting it done within the time limits. These factors mirror the components of the strategic mindset and are the very factors that have been substantiated as pathways to success in college: self-knowledge, self-advocacy, and initiative in use of support services (Patton & Polloway, 1996; Riley, 1999a; Vogel & Adelman, 1992). (See Appendix D for Checklists of Skills of Self-Advocacy and Self-Awareness).

## Conclusion: *Getting Started*

Best is that students begin to build these areas of the strategic mindset early, and middle school is not too soon to begin the process. Neither is it ever too late to begin. As one college student commented:

> I wish I knew so much about myself in high school. I could have done so much better, but at least I'm learning now...and it doesn't just help with school...it comes up all through my life (Riley, 1998, p. 114).

# Chapter Three

# Preparing Students with Learning Disabilities for College

*William J. Rowley, Ed.D.*
Department of School Counseling and Psychology
Seattle Pacific University
Seattle, WA

*Charles E. Rehberg, Ed.D.*
School Psychologist/Counselor
Sumner Public Schools
Sumner, WA

**William J. Rowley, Ed.D., Charles E. Rehberg, Ed.D.**

Federal law makes it clear that students with disabilities have the right to an education and cannot be discriminated against because of their disability. This includes those students with a learning disability, who by definition have difficulty with academic achievement in one or more areas where a discrepancy exists between their potential for learning and what they have learned. Although implementation of the law can be problematic, their right to an education has been firmly established. A learning disability need not prevent students from fulfilling their educational goals.

When it comes to post-secondary education, having the right to an education is not the full story. The need for learning disabled students and their families to prepare for this different educational experience is critical to ensuring their success. Knowing what services a student needs, which services are available at a particular college or university, and how to access them are important elements of preparing for an education beyond high school.

It is likely that students who have been identified as having a learning disability in a K-12 school setting have experienced support in their efforts to succeed in school. School personnel, families, and community resources have worked together to address the needs of the student. The following vignette illustrates the level of this support.

A student was thought to have average or above intelligence but was having significant problems in reading. Her teacher also reported that she did not seem to be as socially astute as her classmates. The student had received various forms of assistance over the years, but still was not able to perform in the classroom like her peers or as one would expect given her estimated cognitive abilities. During a contact with the student's parents by the school psychologist, it was learned that the student had been born prematurely and that the physician had told her mother that learning problems could present themselves in the future. While the mother was aware of her daughter's reading difficulties, she did not know that her daughter may have a learning disability and that additional services would be available if this were the case. After additional background information was gathered and a multidisciplinary team decided to obtain consent for an evaluation of a learning disability, the student was assessed and found to meet the criteria. A severe discrepancy between her ability and her performance in reading comprehension was documented, and it was established that she needed specialized individual instruction through the Special Education Program. The student was certified as learning disabled, and an Individualized Education Plan was developed and implemented to meet her needs.

This scenario is similar to that which many learning disabled students and their parents experience in K-12 schools. From it we learn the characteristics of the support given to students in a K-12 school system. The teacher alerts the school psychologist regarding the student's inability to perform at a level consistent with her estimated ability.

The school psychologist consults with the student's mother, who presented significant information regarding the student's birth and a doctor's warning about potential learning problems. A multidisciplinary team decides an evaluation is in the best interest of the student, the parents gave permission for the evaluation, and it is completed by the school psychologist and the multidisciplinary team. A meeting is held with the parents, a decision is made regarding eligibility, and if certified, the team develops an Individual-ized Educational Plan to meet the student's needs. A variety of school and community resources are used to implement the plan.

How might this experience differ at the college or university level? Colleges and universities will typically have an identifiable educational services staff, but taking a proactive stance by seeking out those students who have learning disabilities is not required. The student or family must request these services. To complicate matters, some students don't want to be identified in college as learning disabled, and many students don't want their parents overly- involved as an indication of their need to establish independence increases. Many parents will lower their level of involvement in their student's educational experience once their children graduate from high school.

Many professors who are in a position to recognize poor performance are likely to think a student simply doesn't belong in college. Some colleges and university's are not "disabled-friendly" in that they have invested minimal resources towards educational services for students who can benefit from them. Unfortunately, there is often poor communication and coordination between student services and the academic program of a school. Students used to the school taking a proactive role in their education will find the college/university experience significantly different.

This brief comparison between the secondary school and the college or university environment demonstrates the need for adequate preparation in order to be ready for this different experience. Recognizing that the kind of support provided in college may be different, it is important to begin preparing for post-secondary education prior to high school graduation.

Getting Started: A Team Effort

Several principles are necessary for a school to effectively prepare learning disabled students for college. First, this must be an intentional, developmental goal of everyone in the school. This task will not happen by chance. Envisioning these students as capable of succeeding in college is paramount. Helping them transition from high school to college will be far more effective when everyone makes a commitment to help them towards their future educational goals.

Obviously, there are some challenges to overcome. Many learning disabled students have a negative self-image and cannot see themselves in higher education. We know that the special education teacher is working hard just to help students meet required objectives in the curriculum areas in order to graduate from high school. The school psychologist is busy with new evaluations, re-evaluations, and meeting compli-ance requirements. The school counselor in a particular school may have little or no contact with students with special needs. However, these obstacles can be overcome by everyone intentionally investing in the future of these students and committing to the following beliefs:

- All students can and do learn.
- Learning-disabled students can and do succeed in college.
- Preparing for college will increase the likelihood of success.
- Preparation will be most effective when it is viewed as a developmental task.
- The most effective way to prepare students for college is when everyone contributes to this goal.

Second, educators need to have an awareness of those areas that contribute to success in college. For example, poor short-term memory, lack of organizational skills, an inability to generalize, inadequate social skills, and an inability to recognize clues for success are all obstacles to succeeding at the higher education level. Recognizing these characteristics serves to identify those areas in which preparation is essential. Improving these skills will certainly go a long way in helping students have a much more positive experience in college. Lacking them is likely to lead to failure.

Third, all school personnel need to recognize they have a role and responsibility in accomplishing this task: students, parents, teachers, administrators, school counselors, school psychologists, and other support staff. For example, a student in college must be able to organize her or his time, tasks, and materials in order to succeed. Someone can teach these skills, but everyone can model them for students.

The part each member of the school staff plays in making sure students have the tools they need in order to succeed in post-secondary education is important. Some tasks like teaching important social skills may appear more significant and substantive. However, others that are more practical are just as important. If a hall pass is required to come to the office, which is analogous to a college professor saying you must have registered in order to attend the class, then the secretary can make sure the student has a hall pass prior to any help being given. We are not helping students when someone teaches the importance of following directions and procedures while others undermine its importance. Students need to be taught specific skills to use when they are on their own in college, and this task will be accomplished more effectively when each person contributes to this goal.

A fourth step in helping prepare learning disabled students for college is for the guidance team to approach this task using a developmental, systemic, intervention model. The American School Counselors Association's *National Standards for School Counseling Programs* (Campbell & Dahir, 1997) and its policy statement on comprehensive counseling (ASCA, 1993) strongly support a comprehensive school counseling program in grades K-12. As of 1996, forty-three states had adopted some form of comprehensive guidance. The guidance staff of every school would be wise to move in this direction for the benefit of all students. Such guidance programs have the following characteristics (Borders & Drury, 1992):

- Counseling and guidance is a distinct, comprehensive program rather than a set of services.

- The counseling program is both an independent and integral part of the total educational program of the school.
- Successful counseling programs are founded on human developmental theories.
- Effective counseling programs serve all students.

Gysbers and Henderson (1994) have created a developmental, comprehensive guidance model for delivering services to all students. A guidance curriculum, individual planning, crisis intervention services, and system support serve as the structural elements of the model. The first two components will be of great assistance in helping learning disabled students gain those skills needed for success in school, in college, and in life.

Underlying the guidance curriculum component is the assumption that there are identifiable competencies that all students need to master in order to be successful in school and prepare for college. Using a developmental model such as this one, guidance counselors identify needs of students, develop a curriculum for meeting those needs, implement the curriculum, and evaluate the program. Since the program serves all students, this curriculum can be used to teach those skills needed by learning disabled students and others to be successful in college: organizational skills, study skills, social skills, time management, and others. As the need becomes apparent, counselors will conduct a unit that specifically covers what students need to know in order to apply for college. Knowledge and skills in these areas will be presented in classrooms or small group settings.

The individual planning component includes all those activities that help students in educational, occupational, and career planning, decision-making, and goal setting. These activities take place one-on-one between the student and counselor and include assessment of individual needs, advisement, and placement. Students can expect counselors using a comprehensive, developmental, intervention model to provide significant, individual help in preparing for college.

Finally, every team member needs to know how to effectively work with these students as they seek to help them prepare for education beyond high school. Suggestions include:

- giving students verbal information about college in small segments.
- providing them with a hard copy of any information given verbally.
- suggesting where students should keep information given in writing.
- repeating information given previously.
- providing reminders to students in a calm and respectful manner.
- recognizing the importance of positive interactions between students and staff.
- helping students meet learning goals by serving on a transition team.
- assisting them by establishing a time frame that identifies the responsibilities of all parties and when they are to be completed.

Knowing students personally, interacting with them in a positive manner, and knowing how these students learn can go a long way in helping them prepare for college. The idea is to have everyone working in concert for the benefit of students who desire to

continue their education by attending a college or university.
Preparation Strategies

One of the underlying principles of a systemic, intervention approach is that individuals impact an entire system (i.e., family, school, community), and the system influences the individual. Circumstances are the result of patterns of interactions among those in the system and are best resolved by everyone in the system getting involved in finding solutions or creating positive changes (Carns & Carns, 1997). The goal of an intervention team is that everyone working together can succeed where one person working alone may be unable to reach the goal. Regardless of one's role, each person can contribute to the preparation of students for college. No role is too small or too insignificant. Working together, the student and each intervention team member can greatly improve the student's chances for success in college.
Roles and Responsibilities

The learning disabled student must be actively involved in the process of seeking and acquiring the knowledge and skills necessary to succeed in college. Interestingly, the coordinator of disability services at one university in the Northwest suggests that students with learning disabilities who have been working as a member of an intervention team in high school tend to make better use of available educational services in college. They have accepted responsibility for their education and have learned to take advantage of all of the services the school and community provide. This knowledge can be taken with them when they go to college.

An important part of this new responsibility is for learning disabled students to begin advocating for themselves. This is developmentally consistent with the fact that teenagers are maturing into young adults. Asking for help in preparing for college from school personnel will ensure that they get the help they need. Advocating for themselves will also assist these students tremendously upon arriving on a college campus. As has been mentioned previously, educational services must be provided at the college level, but there is no requirement for staff to seek out those students with special learning needs. These services must be requested.

Once the student has graduated and entered college, school personnel in a high school cannot be expected to advocate for these students forever. And, students themselves generally want their parents to back off from running interference for them. Unless they begin to accept responsibility for their own education and seek out all services to which they are entitled, they may not receive the level of help they need in order to succeed.

Although increased responsibility by students is important, they must be provided with the necessary tools for such action by school personnel. For example, students can receive assertiveness training in a small group conducted by a school counselor. Through the means of role- play, they can practice requesting assistance from the educational services unit of a particular college. Or, they can complete a writing assignment under the supervision of a special education or English teacher informing a college or university of his or her specific needs upon arrival on campus.

As a student, you will want to:

- Tell your teachers and counselor you want to attend college following high school graduation. You can succeed if you prepare for it. Don't be afraid to ask questions. College is a different world, and you aren't expected to know all about it.
- Learn about your strengths and weaknesses. Your teachers and counselor can help you identify them. For example, you might need to learn how to organize your time and materials. Don't let this information discourage you. School is all about helping you prepare for the next step.
- Find out about one-on-one and small-group opportunities at school that can help you work on those areas of weakness that are important for success in college. Sign up for and attend these opportunities. Take full advantage of them and do your best to learn all you can. It is the key to your successful future.
- Ask your school counselor or the coordinator of your school's career resource center to give you information about colleges that might fit your needs. Ask them specific questions. For example, you might want to ask:
    Where do I find out information about colleges?
    What are the requirements to get into college?
    How do I apply to college?
    Who can help me complete the application?
    When do I apply to college?
    What skills do I need in order to succeed in college?
    Who can help me learn these skills?
- Share all of this information with your parents. They care about you and can help you sort it out.
- See your teachers, school counselor, and others as people who want to help you. They won't make decisions for you, but they can help you figure out what you want and need to do.
- As a goal in your Individualized Education Plan, work with your special education or English teacher to develop a plan for entering college that includes the writing of a letter to the college or university to which you have been accepted outlining your needs and the help you wish to receive upon your arrival on campus. Remember, you are entitled to assistance from the ages of three to twenty-one.

Parents are in a difficult position as their children begin the transition from high school to college. On one hand, it is not helpful to stop providing support and assistance to those children who desire a college degree simply because they have graduated from high school. College is a different environment and there are new expectations that are unfamiliar to them. On the other hand, students need to separate and figure out who they are apart from their parents. They need to grow and mature into independent individuals in their own right. College is a good place to do that.

The task of parents is to work *with* rather than for their children when it comes to helping them prepare for college. Students need to learn new skills and use them in college when their parents are not around. Abandoning them completely to this new experience will put them at a disadvantage when it comes to familiarizing themselves with the college scene. The idea is to help them gain the skills they need, and give them opportunities to practice them.

As a parent, you will want to:

- Continue your support and assistance as your young adult begins the transition from high school to college. However, be aware that your child is going to want more independence as he or she approaches college age. This is normal and developmentally appropriate. Encourage your child to be involved in the process.
- About the junior year, talk to key teachers and the school counselor about your child's desire to attend college. They can begin providing information and experiences that can help your child meet her or his goal. Ask how they can help and what you might do to facilitate the process. Find out what steps your child needs to take in order to make this goal a reality.
- Encourage your child to take advantage of the knowledge and experience of school personnel. Teachers and school counselors have a wealth of information that can help your child prepare for college. Be specific, and don't do things your child is capable of doing. For example, you might want to say to your child, "Today, ask your counselor what the first step is in applying for college. Let's talk about what she tells you when you get home."
- If you get a permission slip informing you that your son or daughter has been selected to participate in a particular learning experience (i.e., how to organize, study, meet new friends), be supportive. Do what you need to do to make this happen. These activities will help your child prepare for college.
- Ask your child's teachers and school counselor for recommendations. They may know the perfect place for your son or daughter to attend college. Remember, they are there to help.
- Call the educational services unit of any college or university your child and you are considering. Begin developing a relationship with the staff so they are familiar with the needs of your child before he or she arrives on campus. The staff's response will help you determine if the campus is "disabled friendly." See if the school has invested in helping students with special needs. For example, is there an individual who is the coordinator of disabled services? Find out what services are provided and determine if they are appropriate for your child. You also can find out what kind of documentation they will need in order to design a program that will address your child's specific learning needs.
- Give permission for key school personnel to communicate with a college or university about your daughter or son. For example, they can send a copy of

the Individualized Education Plan and a recent evaluation to appropriate disability services staff but only with your permission.

The <u>school administrator</u> has a key role in determining the educational mission of the school. Certainly, it should be the school's overall mission to prepare all students to develop their full potential. The role of the principal is to assist teachers and students to meet the educational objectives developed by the school district on behalf of the community. Although contact with students may be indirect, the direction and tone is often set by the administrator who has responsibility for the education of all students of the school.

If you are a school administrator, you will want to:

- Support the efforts of teachers, students, and families to prepare for success beyond high school. See Special Education as an intervention, not a destination.
- Get to know students with special needs in your school as well as those in the regular education program.
- Encourage learning disabled students to fulfill their full potential. When you see them, talk to them about their plans upon high school graduation. Ask if they are considering further education. They may not all go to college, but you may be planting a seed. It may encourage a student to know that you believe college is a viable option for them.

The <u>school psychologist</u> plays an important role in the life of students with learning disabilities. It is this school professional who helps determine the student's eligibility for placement in Special Education. More importantly, it is the school psychologist who in consultation with parents and other school personnel helps develop learning objectives in an Individualized Education Plan. Succeeding evaluations determine the effectiveness of a program designed to meet these objectives and may suggest placement in regular education classes.

If you are a school psychologist, you will want to:

- Encourage other school personnel to see Special Education as an intervention rather than a destination. Its role is to provide interventions that effectively address the the needs of a particular student. Successful interventions can and do lead to growth and development of the student.
- Help others recognize that students with learning disabilities can and do succeed in college. Other school personnel and families may not know this.
- Collaborate with the Special Education Teacher, regular education teachers, school counselors, families, and others to develop objectives that will help students directly or indirectly prepare for college.
- Participate in the development of the student's transition plan as she or he moves through high school as required by the Individuals with Disabilities Education Act .
- Encourage learning disabled students to think about what they want to do after high school graduation. If appropriate, ask them if they are considering college.

Teachers as well as others so designated will continue to help students meet objectives in Individualized Education Plans. Successful completion of these objectives and high school graduation help learning disabled students become eligible for college entrance. Preparing them for college is an intervention, and the Individualized Education Plan of any student planning to attend college should include interventions that assist her or him towards this goal.

These students' teachers will be of great assistance in this task. Since they have a clear grasp of the student's strengths and weaknesses, they can address these needs and direct students to resource people on campus and to opportunities at school that can help them toward their educational goals. Believing that learning disabled students can succeed in college with adequate preparation can do much to encourage them to enroll in college.

As the special education teacher, you will want to:

- Encourage your students to consider receiving a post-secondary education. Learning disabled students can and do succeed in college, and they may need to know that you believe in them.
- Help your students identify those areas of weakness they need to address in order to succeed in college. Direct them to people, activities, and opportunities at school and in the community that can help them learn the skills they need.
- In multidisciplinary team meetings, recommend objectives that will specifically address skill areas needed for success in college.
- Collaborate with the school counselor, the school psychologist, and any other school personnel who can help the student and his or her family to successfully navigate all the details for college selection and entrance.
- Continue to determine when it is appropriate to assign students to regular education classes. Recommend which classes and which teachers would be most beneficial for the student. For example, if you determine that a student needs to learn organizational skills, a skill that is important in college, it would be a good idea to place her or him with a teacher who models excellent organization.
- Consult with teachers in the regular education program regarding the special needs of learning disabled students, and share instructional strategies that have proven to be effective with these students.

School guidance counselors are positioned to be of great assistance to all students who need to prepare for college. Their role, functions, training, and experience all point to helping students get ready for life beyond high school. Unfortunately, a high student load (anywhere from 400 to 900 students), administrative duties (discipline), scheduling, and paper work can be overwhelming. An attempt to see each student one-on-one becomes almost impossible. Instead of anticipating the developmental needs of their counselees, they must guard their time for those things that have immediate urgency. After all, every student must be in a class every period!

The belief by some that school counselors are not always available or helpful to every student is not new. However, a major turning point occurred in the 1960's with the development of a comprehensive guidance model. Norman Gysbers, a major contributor to this idea found that school counselors had "solid program ideas," but organizational structures in which they worked made it difficult to put those ideas to work and at times were counterproductive. This resulted in their becoming managers and administrators rather than student developers (Good, Fischer, Johnston, Jr., & Heppner, 1994).

The comprehensive guidance model described above is an approach for more effectively delivering guidance services and addressing the developmental needs of all students. This includes preparing students for college if that is the educational goal of the student and his or her family. Rather than every student visiting the counseling office, counselors go where students are. Through classroom guidance lessons, small skill-building groups, and individual planning, school counselors are able to address the developmental needs of all students, including preparation for future educational experiences. Students with learning disabilities have every right to benefit from the efforts of school counselors in their quest for a college education. This improved organizational structure for delivering guidance services to all students means that these students can benefit from the knowledge and expertise school counselors have about college.

If you are a school counselor, you will want to:

- Work with your school administration and school personnel to develop a developmental, comprehensive guidance model. You may have already done this. If not, this approach will enable you to more effectively use all the knowledge and skills you have for the benefit of all students. You may want to obtain a copy of *Sharing the Vision: The National Standards for School Counseling Programs* (Campbell & Dahir, 1997) from the American School Counselors Association. You may also want to read what leading counseling professionals have written about the characteristics of developmental comprehensive guidance (Borders & Drury, 1992) and how to implement such a program (Gysbers & Henderson, 1994).

- View special education as an *intervention*, not a destination. It is important to work with all students to prepare them for life beyond high school.

- Make a special effort to work with the families of students with learning disabilities. Although some parents may be familiar with selecting and applying to college, many parents will be completely unfamiliar with and anxious about the process. They need to be an integral part of the process, and they will need to know what their role is in helping their children prepare for college. When appropriate, help them make contact with the educational services unit of any college or university their son or daughter is considering.

- Recognize that students with learning disabilities can and do succeed in college. Work with them one-on-one and include them in your small skill-building groups so they can get the preparation needed for college. Use teaching strategies that are effective. Encourage and help them toward their goal.

- Appreciate the fact that you will need to work with these students in a manner that recognizes their special characteristics. As noted above, you will want to give verbal information in small "chunks," provide a hard copy of information you have given them verbally, tell them where to store this information, and repeat information in succeeding contacts.
- Give students with learning disabilities "tips" for success. For example, tell the student to always type a college application. Or, tell the student to find out which of their professors in college require you to bring your textbook to class. These suggestions for success counter the student's inability to pick up on clues.
- Collaborate with the Special Education Teacher, regular education teachers, the school psychologist, and others to identify what the student needs to prepare for college. Determine how the guidance program can best address these areas.

Other school personnel can have a part in preparing students with learning disabilities for college. For example, a school secretary can provide opportunities for students to apply skills they are learning from teachers, school counselors, and others. A secretary who is informed that a particular student is learning to follow directions can make sure the student applies this knowledge in the school or counseling office.

If you hold a staff position in the school, you will want to:

- Get acquainted with as many students in your school as possible. Recognize Special Education as an *intervention* designed to help students develop their full potential. Ask students what they plan to do after high school. Let them know that students with learning disabilities can and do succeed in college. Encourage them to work with their teachers and school counselors towards this goal.
- Let teachers and school counselors know you are willing to contribute to the development of students with whom you come in contact. Give examples of how you might help a student apply what he or she is learning in the classroom.

Finally, some parents will retain the services of an independent education consultant, a person not employed by the school but who has special expertise in helping students with learning disabilities. If a family turns to someone outside of the school to help their child prepare for college, it is important for that person to obtain permission to work closely with school personnel in order to provide an integrated effort on behalf of the student.

Summary

Students with learning disabilities have the right to a college education. However, to ensure their success if this is their goal, they need to begin preparing for this new and different experience in high school. The goal of preparing for college will likely be accomplished when everyone, students, teachers, administrators, the school psychologist, the school counselors, secretaries, and others, all work together.

Preparing students for college will also be much more effective when the task is approached through a developmental, systemic, and intervention approach using a comprehensive guidance model for delivering services to students. Students with learning disabilities can and do succeed in college. As they prepare for college, their chances for success at this educational level will be greatly enhanced.

# Chapter Four

# What is a Parent to Do?
# The Parents' Roles in College Planning
# for Children with Learning Disabilities

*Leslie S. Goldberg, M.Ed., CEP*

**Leslie S. Goldberg, M.Ed., CEP**

As parents we have always tried to advise, encourage and help our children the very best we could. Parents of children with learning disabilities have historically gone above and beyond others, feeling that their children needed more support. Very often this, in fact, has been true. There comes a time, however, when that help can be counter-productive. As students approach the time to prepare for college or other post-secondary options, they need to learn how to become independent, since parents are not with them in college. In addition, children and adolescents often develop a *learned helplessness* when parents continue to do too much for them. It is almost as if you are telling him he doesn't have the ability himself. Think carefully about this. How will he ever learn to be independent? If a child has to encounter difficulty, it is better to have it happen now when he is under your roof! He will learn, even through trial and error, to stand on his own two feet! His self-esteem will grow by leaps and bounds because he is actually doing this on his own, without you, the parent, as a crutch!

What does that mean for parents? How do we step back in a way that our children won't fall on their faces?

- First, parents need to begin a positive feedback and encouragement campaign. A pat on the back accompanied by a "You can do it!" often works wonders for self-esteem and motivation.
- If you have been in the habit of helping with homework, it is time to stop. Yes, stop! Right now! If s/he needs assistance, extra help is always available after school; a tutor may be hired; another student in the class might offer to help; or more help from an aide in the classroom might be available. Never, never, never do your child's homework for him! How will he perform on a test in class without you there?
- Brainstorming with the child about how best to do an assignment or how to come up with a topic for a research paper is appropriate support. Doing it for him is not.
- Allowing the student to do his own work doesn't eliminate you from the education loop. It is a good idea to tell the teachers, guidance counselor and special education director that you are backing off in order to strengthen your child's independence, but need to be informed when things are not going well before it is too late to bring up a low grade!
- Weekly or biweekly reports might be a good idea so that the parent is on top of what is happening (or not happening) in school. This also helps the student have a good idea of how he is doing so there won't be any surprises at the end of the term.
- Pretend you are at an expensive boarding school, with quiet study halls from 7:00 to 9:30 p.m. Sunday through Thursday nights. Do not allow phone calls, music, television, Internet or computer games during that time.

In addition to the parents' backing off, the students need to learn how to become more independent. Teach your child to become a strong self-advocate and to be assertive without acting entitled or demanding.

- Have the student practice explaining his particular type of learning disability and learning style in his own words. If he doesn't have a clue what "auditory processing" means, have him practice stating that he has a hard time taking notes in a lecture or remembering assignments given verbally, for example.
- The student should meet with the teachers one-on-one at the beginning of each term or semester so that they will understand what he may need in the way of accommodations. Even teachers who mean well can forget such things from time to time and a meeting can help alleviate any problems or misunderstandings later on.
- Make sure that the testing (psychoeducational or neuropsychological) is up to date so that accommodations are clearly spelled out. The tests must be done within two years of application and should include a Wechsler Adult Intelligence Scales III, a Woodcock-Johnson Achievement Test-Revised, and any other instruments suggested by the examiner. The Wechsler should be the adult version, and can be done only after the student is about sixteen and one-half years old.
- The testing should clearly explain any strategies and/or accommodations so that colleges will know easily if they can offer appropriate support. This also helps the student know what he should have available to him at the high school and the college level.

Although by law (current at the time of the writing of this article*) all colleges accepting federal funds must accommodate students with special needs so that there is a level playing field for all students, not all colleges or universities do this well. It is up to the student to interview the support staff to find out if the accommodations suggested in his testing will be available at a particular institution. Then if he is accepted and matriculates at the college or university, he must self-advocate for these accommodations. No one will come after him! This is why students must be such strong self-advocates before they leave for college.

It is also important to self-disclose in the college admissions process, if the student was identified in the high school setting. If he does not, and later needs accommodations, it is more difficult to accomplish after the fact. Furthermore, if any testing is required for competency exams for a particular major, no accommodations will be allowed unless the student has self-identified as learning disabled.

If there is a question as to whether or not the college will accept the student if he self-discloses as learning disabled, just ask yourself the question: If they don't accept me because I have a learning disability, why on earth would I want to be there in the first place? How uncomfortable would it be if they did not accommodate students with learning disabilities, and I was a student there?

Independence must be practiced in the living skills as well. Adolescents who have had their clothes picked up from the floor, been given money as needed, and told what to

---

* for the most up-to-date information, check with the Association for Higher Education and Disability in Boston.

eat and when to eat it should begin practicing some of these skills in addition to the others:

- Have the student get a part-time job. This will help with time management and responsibility.
- Start a checking account for the student. He will need to learn how to budget and pay bills. At least this way you can make sure of his skills before he is entirely on his own.
- Have your student do his own laundry, at least the underwear, T-shirts and jeans. If the underwear turns pink or gray a few times, the expensive stuff is less likely to get ruined.
- Give your student some responsibility with selecting, shopping for and preparing meals. He will be thankful when he is on his own in college. Students in this day and age usually eat college food only their first year or two.
- If possible give your student a credit card with a small limit on it. Students are bombarded with credit card offers in college and many get themselves very heavily into debt. If they have some experience with paying bills and understanding what can happen with high interest building up, they will be safer later on.
- Parents should be sure that their children are extremely well versed and comfortable with computers. Not only will they need to do word processing, but many professors post their messages to the students by e-mail or on the college's web site. If the student has no clue about computers (hard to believe in this day and age, but possible) get some very good instruction quickly!
- Parents might want to invest in a study skills course during the high school years. Students who can't manage their time or take good notes will be lost in college.

College is expensive, and most parents want their children to be prepared for the world of work when they graduate. It is therefore a good idea to plan ahead for career choices and the realities of the job market while still in high school.

- Having your student take a Myers-Briggs Personality Type Inventory is a good idea to see what kind of job might fit his personality. It is not only fun to do, but it is also an eye-opener for parents who have felt their children should fit a certain mold. A full-blown career inventory isn't necessary at this point in time, but the MBTI is worth considering.
- See if your high school offers a shadowing or mentoring program for various kinds of careers. If they do, encourage your children to take part, because only after following someone around for a day or a week can one actually see what a specific job entails.
- If your high school doesn't offer such a program, try to start one or find a friend in a job that your child indicates an interest in and ask if he might shadow the friend. Why go for a four-year degree in a major the student ends

up disliking due to the type of everyday work?

- The shadowing experience should allow the student to see the good, the bad and the ugly about the job. If an exciting picture is portrayed, and reality is very different day-to-day, he will be disappointed and not last in that career.

Parents should encourage their children to challenge themselves in areas other than just academics. If they have gifts or talents in the arts or in athletics, these students should try to attain some leadership positions if at all possible during high school. This will lay the groundwork for both college and life and naturally build self-confidence.

Extracurricular activities as well as courses should demonstrate depth and breadth, and should enable the students to become passionate about some part of their high school careers. Parents should oversee that this is possible.

As much as the parents should let go of some of the academic issues, it is the their responsibility to oversee their children's college admission and application process. This does not happen on its own. If you leave this up to the adolescent, who in most cases will put his head in the sand until the tide washes over it, he will not have the options he might otherwise have. Start the process early enough that you have a handle on what you are doing; this is perhaps one of the most important decisions your child will make.

As early as ninth grade parents should encourage the most challenging courses (as long as there are no final grades of C or below!) and a selection of activities that will span the four years of high school. This will fulfill the "depth and breadth" mentioned previously in this chapter. "Well-rounded" isn't the phrase of choice in the 21st century college admissions. Rather, the colleges like to see passion about a few interests and great depth.

Course selection is very important because the range of college options will be impacted if the following courses are not taken when considering competitive four-year colleges and universities:

- 4 years of English
- minimum 3 years of math (4 is better)
- 3 years of science (4 is better)
- 3 years of history or social sciences (4 is better)
- minimum 3 years of foreign language (4/5 is better) If the foreign language has been waived due to the learning disability, either sign language or a culture course or an immersion program would be recommended.
- computer course
- performing or visual arts

If the student is not considering a competitive four-year college or university and opts instead to go to a community or two-year college, these are not as important. If the disability is in the math area, and only three years of math is possible, it is important (even if tutoring is necessary) to at least try to get to Algebra II.

In addition to the course selection and levels, summers should be well planned. Many students have to work; yet even with a full time job, a course in an area of strength can be taken at a local community college. If the student has an area of weakness (e.g.

foreign language) this is also a good time to take a course because it is only one course at a time, without the distractions of several other courses.

If the student doesn't have to work the whole summer, he can select a summer enrichment program at a school or college campus. This option would offer an opportunity to take courses in the academic arena or in the arts. In addition, there are wonderful opportunities for community service projects. These are not just to fill in the college applications, but to allow adolescents to feel really good about helping others less advantaged than they. Some students select travel programs or outdoor leadership treks. Since most programs offer scholarships, there are few reasons not to consider some of these options.

School vacations, as early as ninth grade, are a great time on a family vacation for students and parents to tour colleges. It is then, before the time pressure is looming, when the family can leisurely get a feel for large or small, urban or rural, research university or liberal arts college. Do not just do "drive-throughs," however. Take the *real* tour through the admissions office, calling ahead to find out when they are offered, and fill out the information card in the office. This will automatically place the student on a mailing list and the appropriate materials will be sent in a timely manner. As a matter of fact, between junior and senior year, you'd better get a very large mailbox!

After getting a feel for the type of campus at which the student feels most comfortable, it is time to get some help from the guidance counselor or the educational consultant to put together a reasonable list of about twenty colleges or universities to start visiting and interviewing. This should happen during the second half of the junior year, after the PSAT scores have been received, and after most of the college applications for the seniors have been submitted and some decisions already made. Certainly, if an early action or early decision application is to be considered, the family must have done its homework before the senior year begins. These applications are submitted by November of the senior year and the decisions are sent by mid-December. Early action is not binding, and early decision is binding, meaning that if one is accepted at an early decision college or university the student is morally and ethically bound to attend.

"Interviewing?" you ask. "I thought they don't interview any more." Well, even if the college doesn't officially offer interviews, it is your job to find out as much as you can from not only the admissions officers, but from the learning disabilities support staff (if there are some) and from professors or heads of departments. It is therefore quite important to interview the colleges you are most serious about. They aren't just interviewing the student; the student is interviewing them to make sure that the fit is right.

Post-secondary institutions offer various levels of support in their L.D. programs. Some are full, comprehensive programs and include a director as well as specially trained master's level instructors. Others have smaller supportive programs with tutors without special education training. Still others offer support and accommodations only. It is the job and responsibility of the parents to determine that the support is appropriate for their children. Once the student matriculates at his choice institution it is then the responsibility of the student to self-advocate to ensure that this continues

Do not think even for a minute that you can simply go to a college guide for students with learning disabilities and select your colleges that way. By the time the guides are in print, two years have gone by, and the information most likely is no longer accurate. It might be a good starting point, but then at the very least, go to the colleges' web sites and do more research there. At least the information is current. The web sites as well as the view books, are marketing tools, and are designed to attract your interest, not to enable your student to be admitted or thrive! The only way to do this is to actually pound the pavement at each college, do your due diligence, or *caveat emptor* (buyer beware.)

Would you ever consider buying a car without test-driving it? This is a more expensive item than a car and certainly has more impact on the student's life. You absolutely, positively must visit! An article by Richard Gustafson in the Boston Globe (March 26, 2000) titled "Don't choose a college without kicking the tires first" offered the same advice, suggesting strongly that parents do their "due diligence."

- Make sure that you plan enough time on each campus, at least two to three hours, depending on how many people you have made appointments with.
- Most admissions interviews last 30-45 minutes, and most tours last an hour.
- Leave time to grab a snack in the campus hangout or dining hall so that you can observe the student in what could be his home for four or five years.
- Do these students look like they could be my child's friends? Does he look comfortable here?
- A really good indication of comfort is if the child leaves the parents staring at each other while he takes off around the campus! Don't worry; he'll be back.
- Check out the library. Is it being used? Are students studying or simply hanging out? Very often the first floor allows talking, but higher floors don't, so don't judge by just the first floor. Are small study rooms available, or study carrels (desks with distraction-free panels on three sides) available?
- What is the town like surrounding the campus? Is it safe? Are there things to do? Does it appear that the locals resent the students? (This is often referred to as "town-gown relations.")
- You may have always dreamed of your child at a rah-rah football type of university, yet that might not be what feels best to him. Remember who is going to college — not you!
- You might feel the college is run-down, too modern or too old fashioned. Once again, you aren't the one going this time around (although personally, as I tour one magnificent campus after another, I often wish I could be in college now, there is so much to offer!)
- Around campus, make sure you check out the bulletin boards. These are a great indicator of what is going on around campus socially and politically. You will know very quickly if the campus is conservative or liberal by checking these out.
- Bulletin boards also usually have a ride board so you can see where the students come from and where they are traveling.

- Look also at the career planning and placement office bulletin board for internships and job offers. You can easily see how available these will be when the time comes for your child.
- Look around to see if students are talking with professors, or meeting with them in offices.
- Do the professors seem approachable? Students with learning disabilities need accessible professors.
- What about a learning center where non-standard tests are to be taken?
- Is there a learning center where help is readily available? Is it a user-friendly place, or is it cold and unapproachable? Are students looking happy and comfortable as they walk in and out? Are students looking stressed and unhappy?

Does the college enable students with learning disabilities to pre-register? Many colleges and universities allow their students with disabilities to register before anyone else to get the courses that they need. If not, how easy is it to get the courses the students would like? As it is, many students need to take a reduced course load, and graduating in five years instead of four is more the norm. If, in addition to a lighter course load, the student can't get the courses he needs, the parents may be looking at more than five years of tuition! Be aware!

We have just gone through the bare minimum of what we, as parents, need to consider as our children head toward college and independence. No one ever said that parenting was going to be easy; after all, children didn't come with a set of instructions! Nevertheless, one of the most difficult tasks is beginning now, as you read this chapter: letting go. I highly recommend a book of the same title written by Karen Coburn from Washington University in St. Louis, Missouri. We have nurtured, watched, taught, and loved these precious children, and now it is time to give them their wings.

The following is a poem given to me in graduate school. Keep this in mind as you "launch" your college-bound children!

*To laugh is to risk appearing the fool*
*To weep is to risk appearing sentimental*
*To reach out is to risk involvement*
*To expose feelings is to risk exposing your true self*
*To place your ideas and dreams before the crowd is to risk their love*
*To love is to risk not being loved in return*
*To live is to risk dying*
*To hope is to risk despair*
*To try is to risk failure*

*But the greatest hazard in life is to risk nothing*
*The one who risks nothing does nothing and has nothing and finally is nothing*
*He may avoid sufferings and sorrow,*
*But he simply cannot learn, feel, change, grow or love.*
*Chained by his certitude, he is a slave; he has forfeited freedom*
*Only one who risks is free!*

Author Unknown

You have come to the point in your adolescent's life when it is time to let go. Give your child the confidence to take risks and fly, and you both will reap the rewards.

# Chapter Five

# Is College Right For Me?

*Barbara Priddy Guyer, Ed.D.*

**Barbara Priddy Guyer, Ed.D.**

John Andrews had never been a particularly good student throughout his years in school in grades 1-12. Now he is a high school graduate, and he must decide "Is college right for me? Or should I get a job immediately after graduation and forget college?" John had received fair grades in school, with a "C" average (2.0) from his years in high school. He had received minimal services from Learning Disabilities Specialists in twelve years, but few teachers had ever given him the help he needed to improve his basic skills in reading and spelling. Mathematics had always been easy for him, and he performed on grade level, if not above on most achievement tests. According to his latest tests, he was reading on a 9th grade level and spelling on a 6th grade level. He knew that if and when he decided to go to college he would need to get remedial help to improve his reading and spelling skills. But would he be better off and happier getting some vocational training instead of going to college? Or should he wait a year before deciding?

Let's review some things that John (and you) should consider before taking the big step and enrolling in college:

**1. Are you a determined student?** Are you willing to work harder than other students to accomplish the same goals? Are you able to resist the temptation of going out with other students to party when they invite you? Do you have the courage (and it takes courage) to respond that you can't go because you have to study for a test the next day?

When you get a poor grade on a test or a report after you have worked very hard, what do you do? Do you make an appointment to talk with your instructor about what went wrong and the options that you have to improve the situation? Or do you disappear from view, hoping that you can vanish into the woodwork with your bruised self-esteem that is crippling you beyond belief? Some students who have LD are very difficult to locate when they are embarrassed because of low grades, and this causes them to lose valuable time — time that they should have spent doing additional studying and attempting to correct whatever it was that made them fail the previous test or report.

Some students are very much aware of how long their friends study for a test. If they study longer than their friends, it is just one more indication that they are inferior to their friends. Does it really matter how long one studies for a test? We are all different, and how long we need to study for a test shouldn't be important. Instead, the results of studying, i.e. the grades received, should be what is significant. Some students have an overwhelming need to be like everyone else — in every way. Any deviation from the norm is not acceptable. When a college student reaches the point where it is possible to say, "This is me. Take it or leave it," then life as a college student becomes much easier.

If you are really determined to succeed in school, you will do everything in your power to improve whatever it was that made you fail. Then you will have a much better chance of succeeding in college.

**2. Do you have good college potential?** We have only been giving IQ tests and assigning intelligence quotients to people for approximately one century. Therefore, it is understandable that our tests lack perfection in some situations. If you received an IQ score that is below average, talk with the psychologist who administered the test. You

60

should read a copy of the report that was written, diagnosing your Learning Disability. Sometimes a psychologist will feel that the IQ scores obtained on a student were invalid for several reasons, which might include: excessive noise in the area where the test was administered; the student wasn't feeling well; the physical conditions of the room were poor, such as too much heat; the student was uncomfortable with the administrator of the test; the student was extremely restless or seemed to have a short attention span; or the test was not administered in the student's primary language.

When you are evaluated in high school, be sure to ask the psychologist and others who might be involved in the overall evaluation, to state whether they believe that you should attend college, or should you regroup and consider another means of furthering your education, such as attending a vocational school.

Some people feel very strongly that an IQ test may not always give an accurate indication of the student's IQ, especially if the student has a Learning Disability and/or Attention Deficit Hyperactivity Disorder (ADHD). In some instances, the low sub-tests on the IQ test reveal the areas of weakness that the student has that are a part of the Learning Disability, rather than the student's actual intellectual ability. It is very important to remember this. If you are a student who has a borderline IQ and your report doesn't mention the advisability of your attending college, get a copy of your diagnostic report and talk with a skilled psychologist (who has experience in testing and advising people your age) about your going to college.

Since 1981 I have worked with college students who have Learning Disabilities and/or ADHD. I have found that it is not unusual for the student with the extremely high IQ to be unsuccessful in college if there isn't a good work ethic and if self-esteem is poor. On the other hand, the student with the borderline IQ may do reasonably well and graduate if the work ethic is flawless and self-esteem is good. I have known several young men who received IQ scores in the 80s when they were in high school. After reading their psychological reports, one would have thought that they would probably do well to earn a promotion at a fast food restaurant. In spite of this less than favorable prediction for their futures, they were able to become very successful in the top management levels of major companies. A few have become physicians. One became a very successful surgeon after graduating from one of the top medical schools in this country. It is very doubtful that he was able to do this with an IQ of 85. The individuals I know who have become quite successful with IQ scores in the borderline range have two striking similarities: 1) their IQ scores are probably inaccurate; and 2) they exhibit exceptional skills in the areas of diligence, determination and winning personalities. Don't ever let a statement on one report keep you from reaching your goal. Certainly don't let it keep you from at least trying to receive the post-secondary training that you want so badly. If one professional has said that you don't have college potential, consult at least one other person who is experienced in evaluating people in your age group who have Learning Disabilities and/or ADHD. The late Vice President of the United States Nelson Rockefeller was told that he would never amount to much of anything, yet he was able to become Governor of the state of New York as well as Vice President. He could speak five foreign languages but was able to read none of them. It is fortunate that he used the ability that no one else had seen and that he forged ahead to reach his dream. Perhaps you can do that as well!

**3. Is your self-esteem reasonably healthy?** In working with more than 1500 college students with Learning Disabilities, I have felt that the ones who were most likely to succeed academically were the students who had self-esteem that wasn't bruised or bleeding. These have been the students who seemed to be able to "weather the storms" most easily. During times of trouble, they have had the fortitude to "hang in there" and absolutely refuse to give up. When professors told them that they didn't believe they "belonged" in college, these students have thanked them for taking the time to think about their well being. Then they have said to the professor something like , "Sir, what do I have to do to convince you that I do belong in college? My lifelong dream is to graduate from college and become a _____. I simply can't give up. Will you help me? This means more to me than anything in my life." There hasn't been a professor born, who cares about students, who can resist a plea like that. Several professors have called to tell me, after adamantly stating earlier that one of their students should withdraw from school, that they had changed their minds. They had underestimated the students and now firmly believed that they had what it took to become successful professional people. This is all that most professors want. They want to be assured that a student can be a credit to the profession that has been chosen. No professor should help a student to graduate, knowing that failure in that profession is only a matter of time. If you become a college student, it will be your responsibility to convince your professors (and yourself) that you can compensate for your Learning Disability and/or ADHD and that you can be a credit to your chosen profession.

Most students with good self-esteem have parents who have believed in them and have fought for them all the way through school. They have helped their children to see their strengths as well as to understand their weaknesses. They have helped their children not to be ashamed of the fact that they have a Learning Disability and/or ADHD. They have taught their children that being different does not mean that they are less capable of reaching a chosen goal and becoming successful.

Part of the secret here is that the parents themselves have not been ashamed, but not all students are this fortunate. Some students have parents who feel that when their children have problems, it has negative connotations for the parents as well, and they never seem to be able to accept the fact that LD simply means that a person "learns differently." It does not mean that the person cannot learn or be successful. Some of the most successful people in our society have LD. It is my belief that we should refer to Learning Disabilities as "Learning Differences."

If you feel that your self-esteem is poor, my recommendation for you is that you participate in counseling before it is time for you to attend college. Learn to know yourself better, and you will then be more capable of surviving in rough academic seas when you are a college student.

**4. Do you have problems with depression?** Some students who have Learning

Disabilities and/or ADHD seem to find that they become depressed more easily than do their peers. If this describes you, it will be wise to discuss this with your family physician. A college student whom I know rather well has significant problems with depression, especially when he doesn't perform as well academically as he thinks he should. Recently he received a failing grade in a Biological Sciences class. Science is very difficult for this student, but he insisted on taking the class his first semester in college, although he was advised to wait a semester or two. Since he has so little self-confidence about science, we felt that it would be wise for him to prove to himself that he could be successful in college. Then, when he has a few good grades under his belt, it would be wise to enroll in a freshman science class. Like many students who have LD, he doesn't respond well to suggestions. He is more likely to do what his roommate suggests or someone he has met at a party and hardly knows. This was the case with the class on Biological Sciences. He was in a state of terror most of the semester whenever he allowed his thoughts to wander off to the area of science.

This student received an "F" on a quiz the second week of the fall semester, and instead of telling his tutor about the grade, he lied and said that the quizzes hadn't been returned. Then he said that the professor had lost his quiz, so the professor was going to give him a grade of "A". The student was so embarrassed about the poor grade that he didn't attend class or the laboratory for two weeks. By then he was so far behind that he failed the mid-term exam when he took it a few weeks later. If he had only told his tutor the truth, they could have changed the techniques being used in the tutoring sessions as well as strategies used in studying, etc., and tried to find what might work more successfully. When the student wasn't honest about his failure, he increased the possibility that he would fail the next test as well.

The student became so depressed after failing the quiz and the mid-term exam that he didn't want to do anything but sleep and vegetate. He stopped socializing with the few friends that he had and retreated to his bed, where he felt safe and secure.

You may ask, **"What can I learn from this experience?"** As a high school student, ask yourself if you seem to have problems with depression. If you do, then go to your family physician before you leave for college. Discuss this with your physician, and be sure to do what is recommended. Do not leave for college with untreated depression.

**5. How well do you deal with stress?** If your "steady" of four years finds someone else to be more desirable, if a favorite relative passes away suddenly, what effect will this have on your academic achievement? Of course, this would be difficult for anyone, and it would be normal for a person to want to be alone more than usual, to lose one's appetite or want to eat more than usual, to find it difficult to concentrate, etc. The length of time that this behavior lasts is crucial, however. You can possibly afford to lose a few days of school, but if stress causes you to be absent from class either physically or mentally for longer periods of time, then you are destined for trouble.

If you have had difficulty dealing with stress in the past, then my recommendation to you is that you learn techniques for dealing with stress before you leave for college. There are many books that have been written on the topic of stress, and you may benefit

Barbara Priddy Guyer, Ed.D.

from reading at least one of them (see Recommended Readings).

Take this quick test from *Study Strategies Made Easy: A Practical Plan for School Success* by L. Davis and S. Sirotowitz (1997):

Answer these questions about yourself to see if you are a positive or a negative thinker by checking "Yes" or "No."

| Yes | No | | |
|---|---|---|---|
| ____ | ____ | 1. | I often enter a test situation thinking I am going to do well. |
| ____ | ____ | 2. | I usually start new assignments right away |
| ____ | ____ | 3. | When I write reports I usually like the way they turn out. |
| ____ | ____ | 4. | I am pretty optimistic about my grades on tests and papers. |
| ____ | ____ | 5. | I usually feel good about myself and others. |

If you answered "No" to most of these questions, you can probably use a good dose of learning to think more positively.

Many authors have addressed the importance of learning to think more positively. Norman Vincent Peale was one of the first to do so in his book, *The Power of Positive Thinking*. I have asked many successful professionals who have LD and/or ADHD what was the most important thing that made it possible for them to succeed in an academic setting. It was not at all unusual to hear: "Learning to think positively was the most worthwhile thing you taught me. The negative self-talk that I put myself through on a daily basis was very injurious to my success as a student. I had become my own worst enemy. When I stopped doing that, I began to believe in myself, and I was on the road to success."

Whenever you find yourself thinking negative thoughts about yourself, write them down. Then look at them the next day and try to decide if what you have written is an accurate description of you. For example, you may have written, "I am so stupid. I knew I couldn't pass that test." The next day ask yourself if you are really "stupid." Probably not. Think about why you thought you couldn't pass the test. Also think about how you harm yourself with these negative thoughts. Your subconscious mind responds to every thought you have, whether it is positive or negative. When you are trying to answer a multiple choice question on a test, a little voice inside you may say, "You think it is 'c,' so it must be 'b.' It couldn't possibly be what I think it should be." I have had many students tell me that they have done this many times, only to find that their original thought was the one that was correct. This is just one of the ways in which negative thinking can be harmful to you. Before you decide to attend college, you must begin to get rid of these destructive negative thoughts.

**6. Will you have a problem with independent living?** Some students have been so dependent on their parents during the years when they were in grades 1-12 that it is very difficult for them to live in a dormitory or apartment. Have your parents called you repeatedly to get ready for school, helped you with homework (probably more than they should have), written a great deal of any reports or book reviews that you later submitted as being your own work? If this describes you, begin today by trying to be responsible for getting yourself up in the morning, doing as much of your homework as you possibly can, etc.

Are you familiar with the term, *learned helplessness*? This is the person who has learned to feel that he can do very little without the help of others. It is necessary to have frequent assistance from others, as well as frequent assurance that something is being done correctly. A person arriving at college who has acquired learned helplessness will have many difficult experiences ahead of him until he learns that it is healthier for him to do as much as possible without the help of others.

**7. Do you have problems relating to your peers?** Do you have many (or any) friends? If this is a problem for you, it may be even more of a problem if you live in a dormitory. In group settings, there are usually those who seem to thrive on creating problems for those whom they see as being weaker than they are. Each semester we seem to have at least one student who has his door covered with shaving cream, has prank calls on his telephone at all hours of the night, has embarrassing statements made by others, etc. If you are a person who doesn't seem to relate well to your peers, my suggestion to you would be to seek the services of a counselor or a psychologist who has had experience in working with young adults. Experiences such as role playing can be very effective in teaching a person how to relate more successfully in social situations to one's peers, siblings, teachers, etc. If this is a problem area for you, why not begin getting help now so that when the fall is here, you will have improved significantly. This could make it possible for you to have a much happier school year, and it could mean the difference between whether you pass or fail.

**8. Do you have serious problems with decoding (reading), reading comprehension or written language?** If you do, it will be to your advantage to begin getting remedial help in this area immediately. Work diligently with an LD Specialist throughout the summer months (and preferably longer) before you begin attending college as a freshman. Most of the students we enroll in H.E.L.P. (Higher Education for Learning Problems) seem to have problems with reading comprehension and written language. The majority of our students seem to have the ability to decode words fairly well, but they haven't yet reached the level of automaticity when they read aloud. They often read haltingly, and one guesses from the pained expressions on their faces that they need additional help in this area.

Almost half of the students enrolled in H.E.L.P. at Marshall University participate in our remedial program. I find that professors are much more cooperative when they learn that their H.E.L.P. students are participating in our remedial program. When the professor tells me in a tone that denotes frustration, "Okay, John may have a time extension on his test, but what is he going to do when he goes out into the **real** world?" It helps significantly if I can then tell the professor that we were concerned about that as well, and therefore, we arranged for John to participate in remedial lessons with an LD Specialist. When John graduates from college, it is our hope that he will need few, if any, accommodations in the area of written language.

**8. Have you learned to compensate for some of your learning problems through the computer?** For a person who has problems with written language, the computer is a godsend. The spell check will "catch" many spelling errors, and this may eliminate many of the red marks by your professors on papers that you turn in to them to be graded. There are some errors that the computer will overlook, and it may be wise to have a lowly human proofread your papers to catch those. The grammar check will catch changes of verb tenses in a paragraph, syntax errors, punctuation errors, etc. A few years ago one of our daughters was in law school. She mailed me a copy of a paper that she had written with no assistance from the computer. Also enclosed was a copy of the paper after she had benefited from the services of grammar check and spell check. There was no question as to which was better. In my estimation, the paper she had written by herself was a "C" quality paper, whereas the completed paper that had been reviewed by grammar check, etc., was an "A" quality paper. Grammar check had detected errors that I probably would not have seen.

While you are in high school, take at least an introductory computer class. If possible, take more than that. In my opinion, you will be ahead if you learn to type properly. A good keyboarding class is certainly worth the time that is involved. Being able to type without looking at the keys can save you a great deal of time when you are writing a report.

**9. Have you been exposed to learning strategies and other techniques for making learning easier and faster?** Having a knowledge of outlining, learning strategies, test-taking strategies, etc., can mean the difference between passing and failing a class. Many students who have LD and/or ADHD seem to read words without structuring them, thereby making it difficult, if not impossible, to recall the content later. When you get to the bottom of a page, do you know what you have read, and perhaps more importantly, how the meaning of what you have read can be associated with what you already know? If you can't do this, then you need to get someone to teach you a series of learning strategies so that you can easily recall what you have read and studied when you are taking a test. It is definitely worth the extra time that is involved.

**10. Are you able to communicate with your teachers easily?** Are you aware of the behaviors that seem to displease teachers? If you aren't, you should read about them and be certain that you don't do things such as not looking at the teachers, not appearing to have an interest in the class, coming to class late or interrupting the teacher when she/ he is talking. Do some role-playing with another student, and practice the skills that one needs to have in order to get along well with teachers. If you have problems that you know will offend teachers, go to your teachers and discuss the situation with them. Tell them that you are trying very hard to improve, and you will appreciate it if they will help you. Sometimes preplanning of this sort can prevent a disaster from occurring. You will find that most books on learning strategies for college students have information about this topic.

**Conclusions.** Should you or shouldn't you attend college? That is a decision that only you should make after you have become as well informed as possible. Read any reports that have been written about you, talk with someone who has knowledge of what is required of a college student, and then try to make a decision.

If you don't have the skills now that will be necessary for you to have in college, begin today to try to acquire such skills. Remember, do not let the opinion of one person dissuade you from attending college. My high school counselor told me that she couldn't recommend me for college because my college board scores were low. Today I have a bachelor's degree, two Master's degrees, and a doctorate. I am so glad that I had the courage to ignore the opinion of the counselor and that I did what I firmly believed was the right thing to do. I have often wanted to return to my old high school and wave my degrees in front of her saying, "See, I did it!" If you give it your best shot, I'll bet that you can too.

# Chapter Six

# Questions to Consider
# When Choosing a College

*Rosa A. Hagin, Ph.D.*

Rosa A. Hagin, Ph.D.

The selection of a college is one of the major decisions people make in their adolescent years. It is also one of the major investments of time and money that parents make on behalf of their children. For people with learning disabilities, decisions related to college are particularly crucial. This chapter will raise some relevant questions to be considered in this most important planning process that will have a major impact upon the outcomes in education, vocations, and life adjustment. Because these questions pertain to vital points in the decision-making process, they cannot be answered easily or superficially. Instead they require thoughtful consideration by both student and parents.

Question 1: **Why do I want to go to college?**

Students can answer this question by listing for themselves outcomes that might be expected from education at the collegiate level. They should consider carefully the contribution that post-secondary education might make to their adult lives. It is important also that they admit honestly to themselves negative reasons for going to college, such as the opportunity to live independently away for home or to postpone the major life decisions for an additional two or four years.

Positive answers to this question should dispel any illusions they may have acquired from films or periodicals about the happy, carefree college days in mythical small colleges. These vine-covered pleasure domes probably existed only in the imaginations of the writers. Today most colleges are large, business-like institutions that bear no resemblance to what has been portrayed in those stories. Students who expect "a four year loaf on Dad's dough" may find themselves on academic probation after the first semester and in danger of being asked to leave the campus during the following semester.

Question 2: **What alternatives should be considered?**

Answers to this question would depend to a large extent upon the academic status of the students and the special abilities and skills that they possess. The level of academic achievement will determine to a great extent the kind of colleges students should consider. As part of the transitional planning during the upper grades in secondary school, students with learning disabilities should have a comprehensive assessment of cognitive abilities, educational achievement, psycho-social adjustment and motivational factors. This chapter will provide information for realistic choices among the range of colleges. While the bright, well-remediated youngster should be encouraged to aim toward challenging college programs, the student whose skills are less strong should be advised to be more modest in college choices.

Pre-vocational planning can also be useful in delineating strengths, interests, and special abilities that can highlight a career path for a student. Often students with learning disabilities have strengths that go beyond academic areas that may lead to success in specialized vocational fields such as art, theatre, film, mechanical abilities, photography, computer systems. These special abilities may be significant signals for a career path in later life and should certainly be taken into account during post-secondary school planning.

Matching the students' choices to colleges that provide curricular offerings in these special fields is another kind of answer to this question. Sometimes a four-year liberal

70

arts program may not be the richest setting for the development of these special skills. Alternative schooling might be obtained in schools that provide specialized training in these fields, some of them without regular academic degree requirements.

Transitional planning and evaluation may identify some students who are not yet ready for the academic demands of college. A number of the special schools for children with learning disabilities also provide pre-college programs during the summer or for a post-high school year, as a means of meeting the educational needs of these students. For students with strong intellectual potential but weak academic skills in reading, written language, and mathematics, these programs should be given serious consideration.

Finally, there are some students for whom nearly any college is an inappropriate choice. These people need training in life adjustment skills and rehabilitation efforts to enable them to enter the world of work with good chances for success. A number of these programs fulfill a need for further education for young people with serious learning and life adjustment problems.

Question 3: **Should I consider a two-year or four-year college?**

There are a number of points to consider in making the choice between a four-year program and two-year community college programs. The four year college has the advantage of a continuing program leading to the bachelors degree in a specific area of study. This is the traditional post-high school goal and has the added status that impresses one's contemporaries and their families.

Most colleges make some provision for assistance for people with disabilities, including learning disability. However, the nature of these services may vary in both quality and quantity from institution to institution. Academic counseling by trained counselors is usually available. On the other hand, tutoring may be focused on specific course content and may be provided by other students as part of work-study programs. The student who needs more general help with college level reading skills, time management, organization and writing of term papers may not find it from these students. Furthermore, many four-year colleges are adopting policies that preclude any remedial services at all, because they feel that these problems should be dealt with in other institutions prior to college admission.

Students with a history of a learning disability who look forward to independence as residential students in four-year colleges should also consider that they will be losing contact with the support network that has assisted them throughout their previous schooling. Most professionals know of students who maintained themselves in four-year programs only though faxing drafts of papers for correction by their parents and building astronomical-sized telephone bills as they sought the advice of parents and tutors "back home." All students should consider whether their academic skills are equal to the independent academic demands of a four year college.

For many students with a learning disability, the two-year programs offered in community colleges deserve careful consideration. Although admission to community colleges may lack the status friends and neighbors attach to admission to a four-year institution, these institutions may provide a gradual introduction as a judicious "first step" into higher education. Most community colleges are located within commuting distance from home, so that the support system of parents and tutors is relatively close at hand if needed. Community colleges have accepted the responsibility of providing for special learning needs, often with effective programs for assisting people in developing academic skills at the college level.

Most two-year colleges provide the opportunity for a trial of college work leading to an associates degree. Thus the student who decides college is not for him or her becomes not "a college drop out" but the possessor of an associates degree with training in a specific sequence of course leading to employment. On the other hand, the student with a history of a learning disability who enjoys the challenge of higher education can move on to a four-year college, not only with advanced standing, but also with general skills and work habits that will ensure better chances for success in that environment.

Also to be considered are colleges that have specialized programs for people with learning disabilities. Some colleges enroll as many as fifty per cent of their students with special learning needs. Other programs are organized separately within a college or university with the added option of taking regular courses in specific areas (e.g. mathematics, computer systems) by students who show competence in those areas.

Question 4: **What marketable skills will I have on completion?**

As any college choice is considered, this question should be answered honestly and seriously. A college degree, in itself, does not insure marketable skills. Professionals across the country report the sad stories of young adults who struggled throughout college with marginal grades and many course changes and different specializations to finally achieve a degree. After completing this struggle, they then ask "What shall I be?" They somehow have finished college with such a checkered record that they have not accumulated sufficient knowledge in any specific field. They are wary of the prospect of further study. They have no real goal in mind, yet they are faced with the prospect of earning a living. Such situations emphasize the need for goal- setting as part of transitional planning at each decision-point in education. They also point up the need for searching introspection on the part of the student and careful advising on the part of counselor and parents, so that goal-setting and lifelong planning are dealt with early and effectively.

The college degree is not a goal in itself, rather it is a means of realizing the goals that each student must set for himself or herself after realistic considerations of interests, abilities, and accomplishments.

Question 5: **What kinds of assistance for my learning problems can I expect?**

Federal legislation (The Americans with Disabilities Act and Section 504 of the 1973 Rehabilitation Act) requires institutions of higher education to make provision for people with developmental disabilities. Learning disability is considered one of the conditions to which this legislation applies. Colleges are expected to make "reasonable accommodations" for otherwise qualified individuals. This does not mean that having a learning disability is a "free ticket" around the academic requirements of a college degree. It does mean that, with proper documentation a student, can request some kinds

of assistance. The usual kinds of support for people with documented learning disabilities include:
- extended time on examinations
- help with note-taking in lecture-type classes
- opportunity to use taped textbooks
- access to a learning center with computers
- help with planning term papers
- tutoring in specific courses by student tutors

Both the quantity and quality of services vary widely among institutions; students and their families are urged to check on the nature of supports available during visits to colleges.

Question 6: **How can I document my need for accommodations?**

At most colleges the student services office requires documentation that is within three years of the date of the college application. An informal note from a family physician stating that "applicant has a history of a learning disability and should be granted accommodations" is not sufficient documentation. Admissions offices and student services require formal, factual reports of previous interventions and current status. The current Individual Education Program (IEP), if the student has been in public school, is helpful. There should also be a psychoeducational report with at least the following components:
- a detailed educational history
- educational evaluations of skills in reading, written language and mathematics
- assessment of cognitive functioning
- assessment of motivational and emotional factors

The educational history should contain relevant information to show where the student has been educationally, previous remedial experiences, and where the student hopes to go educationally and vocationally. It should include SAT or ACT scores and information concerning the nature of the accommodations provided when the student attended secondary school.

The educational evaluation should contain achievement test scores for current skills relevant to the goals the student has set for himself of herself. Data in the report should justify any requests for accommodations the student might request. While the choice of measures should be at the discretion of the examiner, the evaluations should report level of word attack skills, vocabulary, reading comprehension and reading rate, spelling ability and mathematics achievement.

Cognitive functioning in terms of well known individual intelligence tests (e.g. The Wechsler Adult Intelligence Scale) and description of strengths and weaknesses that may help a counselor understand the nature of the student's abilities and the impact of the learning disability should be included.

While emotional factors are not the original cause of learning disability, they must be reckoned with in the diagnosis of young adults and the provision of appropriate post-high school educational programs. Information from interview and personality measures

73

are a relevant component of the evaluation. Interest inventories related to vocational planning (such as the Holland's Self-Directed Search) are also useful components of this evaluation.

Reports should conclude with a tightly written summary that recapitulates major points in the evaluation and shows the impact of the learning disability on current functioning. The summary should also suggest specific accommodations that would enable the student to succeed in higher education.

Question 7: **How can I find out which colleges to apply to?**

There are many formal and informal ways to become familiar with colleges. The first of these is through reading. There are published directories of colleges in general, as well as colleges that make specific provisions for people with learning disabilities. (See references for this chapter.) Prospective students can write to request college catalogs. Most secondary school guidance departments maintain libraries of college catalogs to help with this search. Frequently, representatives of admissions departments visit high schools to explain their programs. Some secondary schools hold college fairs. Organizations like the Learning Disabilities Association of America sponsor programs such as the Post Secondary Options Program at the annual meeting. This program brings together representatives of a wide variety of two- and four-year colleges, specialized schools and life adjustment programs.

Less formal sources of information are found among graduates of colleges who are asked by the administration to serve as information sources for prospective students. Current students can also serve as a source of information. However, a major source of information can be found in most secondary school guidance departments. The counselors know about acceptance rates and outcomes of students who have graduated from the school in which they work. Many states require guidance departments to do regular follow-up studies of outcomes at stated intervals after graduation.

After the search has highlighted a reasonable number of possibilities, students should visit the colleges. Obviously, the number of colleges visited is limited by the time and financial resources available to the student and his family, but it must be emphasized that a first-hand view of the college is justified by the crucial nature of this decision.

The visit is particularly important for students with a learning disability because it will give them the opportunity to compare the description of the support services available in catalogs and advertising literature with the actual program currently in operation. It should be recognized that printed materials may have been prepared during the previous year and may not describe services and/or personnel as they are presently operating.

Question 8: **What should we look for in a visit to a college?**

The student and his family should prepare for the visit by reading all available information about the college and by making an appointment to tour the campus and possibly to have an interview. Although individuals differ, most students with a learning disability show up more positively in an interview than in the record of their school grades. However, as application rates have increased, many colleges cannot afford the staff for interviews of all applicants, so this "edge" may not be available at all colleges. Nevertheless, an appointment is necessary if the visit is to be really useful in going beyond a quick tour of campus buildings.

It is important to visit a college when classes are in session. Such scheduling will give the prospective student the opportunity to observe classes in session, visit libraries, laboratories, and computer centers, get some idea of the student body and look at residence provisions and dining arrangements for students. In short, timing the visit when classes are in session will give the prospective student the feel of the college. The prospective student and his family should give consideration to the following points during the college visit:

General Climate of the College

The visitors should spend enough time to get some idea of the size of the student body and the typical class size. Are major courses taught in vast lecture halls? What opportunities are there for tutorials or other kinds of interaction with instructional staff? How large is the number of full-time faculty?

College Curricula

Are the curricula offered in keeping with the interests and abilities of the prospective student? Are opportunities for flexible course loads available for students with learning disabilities? What foreign language and/or mathematics requirements exist on this campus? Are internships or work/ study programs available? How is academic advisement handled? Are taped text-books or taped lectures available in the library? What percentage of the students graduated within five years of entry?

Facilities

Are campus buildings adequate for the curricula offered? Are instructional support services such as libraries, laboratories, computer centers with well-trained consultants available? Is residence space adequate for the size of the student body? Are freshman year students housed on campus? What is the noise level in classroom and residence buildings? (This is especially important for students with attentional problems).

Support Services

What support services for students with learning disabilities are available on the campus? Are there additional costs beyond regular tuition for these services? What is the retention record of this college for students with learning disabilities? Are workshops on time management or study skills available to students with learning disabilities? When tutors are provided, what is their experience in working with people with learning disabilities? Are career counseling, vocational assessment, and job placement services available for students with learning disabilities? Do the counselors help students when they are negotiating accommodations with individual faculty members? What evidence is there of support for programs for students with learning disabilities by the college's administrative officers?

**Summary**

The steps in the search and selection of post-secondary schooling are described here in a series of questions designed to help students and their families think through the choices they need to make in this most important educational decision. Broad questions concerning the motivation for college and the expected outcomes are followed by more specific questions and observations on transitional planning, kinds of assistance needed, documentation, and points to be considered on visits to colleges. Students with learning disabilities should not be discouraged by the complexity of this search, or the variety of choices open to them. They should seek to understand themselves well enough that they can make judicious decisions at each point in the process.

# Chapter Seven

# The Learning Disabled College Student As Leader....A Beginning

*Marsha A. Glines, Ph.D.*

**Marsha A. Glines, Ph.D.**

In 1981 David Elkind introduced us to *The Hurried Child*. He followed this publication with *All Grown Up and No Place To Go – Teenagers in Crisis*. As parents and teachers we read about our parenting and the societal problems resulting from single parents desperately attempting to balance work and family, the impact of television and technology and our fast paced living and learning environment.

In the Preface of *All Grown Up and No Place to Go*, the 1984 publication, Elkind writes about his observations and work with teens and the changes he has observed:

> Over the past two years, however, I have had a very different kind of interaction with teenagers, with their parents and teachers, and with professionals in many different fields who provide for their health needs. With the publication of an earlier book, *The Hurried Child*, I had many requests to speak from all parts of the United States and Canada. I have now traveled to every state in the Union and to all the Canadian provinces. Everywhere I go, I make it my practice not only to speak but also to listen.
>
> What I have heard, and what I am hearing, was the impetus for writing this book. Not only are children still being hurried, but the phenomenon is becoming more common and accepted. Mothers-to-be are deluged with literature assuring them that if they use the right materials they will be able to raise their babies' I.Q. and have them reading, swimming, and doing gymnastics before they are three months old. There is, of course, no evidence to support the value of such early pushing. There is, however, considerable evidence that children are showing more and more serious stress symptoms than ever before. Even more discouraging has been the realization that many of these hurried children are now teenagers. Now, more than a decade after the hurrying began, we are getting a truer measure of the cost of acceleration as we look at the threefold increase in stress symptoms among young people. What I have seen and heard is frightening enough. Many parents and many schools and much of the media have been hurrying children to grow up fast, but they have also been abandoning teenagers. There is simply no protected place for teenagers in today's hurried and hurrying society.
>
> The result is a staggering number of teenagers who have not had the adult guidance, direction, and support they need to make a healthy transition to adulthood. We always lost a certain number of teenagers in the past, for all kinds of reasons. But we are losing too many teenagers today. We are producing too many young people who may never be productive and responsible citizens, much less lead happy and rewarding lives. When 50 percent of our youth are at one or another time abusing alcohol or drugs, then something is seriously wrong with our society.

As we enter the new Millennium many of the children described by Elkind have grown to become the non-traditional students entering our higher education institutions. In the past students entered our colleges and universities as young adults cognitively and socially able to succeed. Rather, today we experience many of our freshmen as "hurried" children, developmentally young, seemingly stuck in the adolescent stage of development they hurried to reach. Their study habits are like those of many adolescents who are unfocused. Their decisions are not always grounded in good thinking and impulsivity often influences common sense behavioral responses to study and living situations. In addition, many of our college students come to us with diagnosed learning disabilities, a history of academic frustration and failure with resulting negative self-concepts. Add to these students' personas the idea, that they are often fearful and uncertain about their futures as discussed in the recently published *When Hope and Fear Collide: A Portrait of Today's College Student* by Arthur Levine and Jeanette Cureton (1998) and we have a challenging and complex group of young people to educate and to help ultimately become our next generation of leaders. During the years between the publications of Elkind and the Levine/Cureton book, educators have been influenced by the publications of Howard Gardner, in particular, *Creating Minds*, (1993) *Extraordinary Minds* (1997) and *Frames of Mind* (1983). It seems that we as educators or diagnosticians could become more successful teachers if we could help our students truly understand themselves as learners. This means helping them understand "the whole" of who they are, cognitively and socially, and the *potential* they have in spite of any issues they bring with them to their college experiences.

In the preface of *Extraordinary Minds*, Gardner concludes that there are varieties of "extraordinary minds" and that each of us has within ourselves "the essential ingredients" to develop meaningful contributions to society. Gardner investigates the idea that there may be traits shared by achievers, leaders, or creative thinkers. "Superachievers," he believes have a special talent for self assessment, the ability to identify strengths and weaknesses. In keeping with this thinking, over the years, many of us in higher education teaching capacities have noted that many learning disabled students do become leaders in college in spite of their cognitive differences, in spite of sometimes unremarkable, unsatisfactory high school academic careers. There are reasons these students ultimately find success in college and emerge as achievers. If we listen and learn from our learning disabled college students who have emerged as campus leaders we can glean an accurate idea of what more we might do to continue to support and encourage all our non-traditional learners to be self-confident and able.

With this in mind, we must consider the 18 year old who is ready to enter college. Who is that young adult sitting in our freshmen classes? Is she the anxious child? Is she the product of our media driven/MTV society? Does she bring learning and social-emotional struggles with her? Does she know what she values, what her future holds? Is she coming to college as the "damaged" child, described in *When Hope and Fear Collide*, with issues involving eating disorders, drug and alcohol abuse, in need of psychological counseling? Is she worried about personal relationships and/or world peace?

Cureton alerts us that students are coming to college less prepared for academics with remedial needs. According to statistics from the National Institutes of Health, one in every five students has a learning or reading disability. If this is true then in every college classroom there are students who process information, and interpret language differently than others.

For us to be effective teachers/instructors/professors, we must genuinely and honestly understand our audience. We must recognize and acknowledge who our students are intrinsically...understand their world views. What are their perceptions? If we allow ourselves to know them, we will understand them. If we understand them, we will teach them. If they trust us, they will allow us to embrace and empower them as life-long learners. We are their role models, all of us who touch their lives. If we can establish a mentoring, understanding relationship with our students, we can help lead them to potential, appropriate, leadership activities on our campuses. It is our responsibility to help them learn about themselves. Trained faculty can do this by providing learning inventories, diagnostic activities and experiences for students to learn about their strengths and weaknesses, aptitudes and genetic dispositions. The more a student understands his/her abilities the better able he/she is to choose an appropriate college major that will lead to appropriate career/employment. This knowledge also provides a structure for the student to investigate and explore leadership possibilities within a major, a future career or within an on-campus activity.

How should we teach students to understand and embrace their non-traditionalism, their learning disabilities so that they become confident, use their creativity and emerge as leaders? Utilizing the work of Howard Gardner from *Frames of Mind*, in terms of multiple intelligence, the strategies set forth by HGSE project zero researchers and personalizing academic assignments help students
- know themselves intrapersonally
- learn to apply support services and resources to build on hemispheric ability
- be better skilled to choose a college major and career
- feel self-assured and knowledgeable and able to take appropriate risks (academically and socially) such as running for student government or participating in on-campus community activities
- identify interest areas that encourage increased content area reading

Using learning inventories, formal and informal assessment and observation, faculty can help students understand and appreciate learning styles and academic strengths and weaknesses. Using an open dialogue approach, teachers can help students assess, discover and experience learning. Achievement is a result of the successful application of cognate skills. Learning for understanding as the Harvard Project Zero folks say.

It is our responsibility to immerse our students in a diagnostic, challenging environment where, ultimately, the student becomes responsible for his/her learning. This is the process. Exposure to self-knowledge. It becomes a gift we offer our students.

Another strategy to help learning disabled college students identify what they value in terms of helping them explore career options and their value systems are the activities introduced to many of us twenty years ago in Sidney Simon's *Values Clarification* and in Leland and Mary Howe's *Personalizing Education*. Activities like the "Pie of Life," "Hex Signs," "Personal Coats of Arms" and "Me Trees" provide self-evaluation opportunities for students to explore what they value. While our students must learn the most current computer applications, it is imperative they also understand who they are, what they value and how this all applies to the potential for lifelong learning, self-fulfillment and leadership. This is a process to help students identify and develop all aspects of who and where they are cognitively and socially.

During fall semester, 1996 a survey was conducted and approximately 40 students, enrolled in EDU 100, Language and Learning Development (a freshman course requirement for learning disabled students entering Lynn University) were asked to respond to questions with input that I hoped would provide me with a clearer idea of what they valued. I hoped to learn about their goals and expectations. I hoped to get a read on who my audience was. Their responses follow:

1.) The students were asked where they hoped to see themselves after graduation and their answers varied immensely.

15 of the students aspired to becoming successful business persons.

7 students hoped to work with learning disabled students in the future.

5 students had no idea as to what their futures might hold

4 students wanted to travel around the world.

3 students planned to settle down, get married, and have children.

3 students wanted to head to the Caribbean and become bar owners.

[Note: I suspect the three students are friends].

4 students wanted to continue their education by enrolling in Master's programs and other post grad options

3 students hoped to become professional athletes (golf)

2 students wanted to go into hotel management.

1 student hoped to give something back to society.

1 student wanted to pursue broadcasting.

2.) The students were asked to identify the five major problems in the world. Many students agreed on very important issues facing our society.

22 students believed that pollution and environmental neglect are serious problems.

20 students were afraid of war and want world peace to prevail.

15 students felt drug abuse is a serious problem facing students today.

16 students were fearful of AIDS and other terminal diseases.

14 students feared violence on the streets.

11 students agreed that racism is a serious societal problem.

10 students felt homelessness is a growing world problem

7 students felt that our government is unable to run the country properly.

6 students were concerned about teen pregnancy and abortion issues.

3 students felt that child abuse was a serious domestic problem.

3 students believed that gender discrimination is a growing problem in our workplace

1 student felt that the current education system is poorly structured and needs to be revamped.

3.) Students were asked if in four years problems in our society would be different than today's problems. Many students had similar pessimistic answers.

21 students felt that societal problems will stay the same, not worsening or improving.

16 students were quite pessimistic and felt that world problems will only get worse and will become more detrimental to our population.

7 students felt that some problems will get solved.

4 students felt that to predict the future is too difficult.

2 students felt that a cure for AIDS will be discovered.

1 students stated that it depends on who is the President of the United States.

1 student believed that the homelessness problem can only improve.

1 student felt that it all depends upon educating society and raising public awareness.

4.) Students were questioned as to what they felt would be worth fighting for in the year 2000. Their answers related to the problems they stated in question number two.

21 students will be fighting for their own success in business and for future happiness.

12 students felt that world peace is an issue worth fighting for.

5 students hoped for freedom among all people in the world.

5 students will work towards economic successfulness.

4 students will fight for health issues, such as cures for AIDS, cancer, and other terminal diseases.

3 students will work to fight drug abuse and the sale of drugs to children on the streets.

3 students wanted to work towards ending homelessness and poverty.

3 students believed that racial issues need to be solved; where all groups can live peacefully together.

2 students wanted to protect children from abuse and to provide them with the rights which they deserve.

2 students could not identify anything they should be working for in the future.

1 student would like to strive for the election of a female president to run our country.

5.) Students were instructed to respond to what they most value in their lives. Several answers were reoccurring.

30 students valued their families and friends as closest to their hearts.

5 students valued their education as an important aspect of their future.

5 students felt all life forms are valuable.

5 students valued their health and happiness.

5 students valued their freedom of choice and their ability to make their own decisions.

3 students valued their cars, for the cars provide them with a mode of transportation.

3 students valued their own determination as a tool for success.

2 students valued imagination as an escape from everyday problems.

2 students felt that honesty is a valuable quality.

1 student felt that the earth is a valuable place with all of its resources.

1 student noted that memories and past experiences are valuable.

6.) When students were questioned about their learning styles and if understanding their individual learning style and cognitive ability was beneficial in helping them succeed, answers were quite individualized in nature.

Several students stated they learn in unique ways, such as hearing books on tape, using visual aides, thus it is critical for them to have this information about themselves. Other students mentioned personal qualities in themselves that help them to excel.

15 students felt that being motivated by a teacher keeps them interested in learning.

8 students were driven by their own self confidence established by knowing as much about themselves as possible.

2 students said they attempted to set realistic goals which are able to be easily met.

1 student felt that common sense guides the learning process for each individual.

1 student responded that understanding where he fit in terms of Gardner's intelligences helped establish and meet goals.

Providing students with an opportunity to explore their values is an effective diagnostic tool. The information gathered and discussed in these kinds of informal questionnaires helped me understand who my audience was. Sitting with each student to discuss how their responses could be connected to interest areas, study/course choices and future work options provided a basis for us to search and discover together. Then, reading Gardner's *Frames of Mind*, and studying the various intelligences while concurrently completing check lists of strengths and likes/dislikes we could together investigate what careers would be appropriate and what work might be most satisfying for each student.

If students expressed an interest in the homeless or other human service area, I could refer the student to the campus group whose community service work involved Habitat For Humanity or the local soup kitchens. We could discuss various related majors including those in Behavioral Science and Human Services. If a student appeared to have the potential to become a social activist, I would encourage the student to become involved in campus politics as well as meet with program advisors in the political science or communication departments. For the student with excellent verbal/expressive communication skills I might walk him/her to the radio station to meet the manager and establish a contact for the student.

It is important to note that I have seen some faculty and counselors initiate these activities. Freshmen Seminar teachers often complete learning inventories with students, advisers often refer students to student services personnel for direction. And, counselors and advisors in the Counseling and Career Center help students investigate career options. This is critical particularly for the group of freshmen who enter universities as "undecided" or "undeclared" majors. Many universities have shared workshops hoping to learn to apply Gardner's research for classroom adaptation. Gardner's work helps us to teach our students about the alternative intelligences.

So many of our learners simply need to be introduced to the idea that their non traditional learning styles may simply mean that are more right hemisphere thinkers – more interpersonal, more physically and spatially able to problem solve. It may be that their linguistic and logical mathematical skills are not their strengths.

We can help predict success by participating as part of each student's social support system. We can and must help them discover, through our informal teaching and diagnostic work, their learning modalities, their value systems and the intelligences that provide their cognitive strengths.

In the Spring and Summer of 1999, I revisited the idea of students having self-knowledge regarding and understanding their learning styles, cognitive ability and values. I wanted to qualitatively examine how some of our learning disabled students became successful campus achievers. Had it been helpful for them to be a part of this discovery/ diagnostic process? What were the influences, patterns or reasons for their success?

Four students who entered our university setting between 1995 and 1996, and who have emerged as campus leaders in spite of their learning disabilities or non-traditional learning styles, were asked specific questions about their academic history, about how four years after the original survey was conducted they overcame academic fear of success, how and by whom they have been influenced. All students interviewed had participated in the first year course, EDU 100, Language and Learning Development, a requirement for learning disabled students, in which Howard Gardner's Multiple Intelligence Theory was introduced, *Frames of Mind* was required reading, and each student's learning style and cognitive ability was evaluated by the student and faculty. The course was designed to empower students with knowledge about themselves as learners. Was the course useful in helping these students identify their leadership potential? Did it encourage them? Could they apply the course information so that they better understood themselves? Or, were there other influences prior to matriculation to the campus? Do they still have the same fears, values, concerns (as they did four years prior)?

David Gill will graduate in May 2000. His major is communications with a minor in business. He is President of the Student Government Association, Chairman of K.O.R. (Knights of the Round Table – service organization), and member of the Greek Expansion Committee. David has spoken as a student representative at campus orientation activities, special events and University Family Weekends. David has maintained a G.P.A. of 3.0.

Jason Laudick is the graduating outgoing, president of the Lynn University Student Government Association. As President he took a stronger look at student rights. His other campus activities included membership in the Substance Abuse Committee and Technology Committee. Jason was a featured student speaker at Families Weekends and at other official University activities.

David Hull graduated in May, 1999. Dave became General Manager of WLYN, the new radio station on campus. As the manager, David supervised and trained 37 individuals associated with the station. He began operating the station with 7 people, implemented many types of programs, including a news department and raised money (locating gifts) to upgrade the equipment for the station.

Ben Tubbs also graduated in May 1999. An international communication major, Ben earned a 3.2 CUM. Sports Editor of the Pulse (Lynn's newspaper), Ben also worked for LUTV (Lynn's television station). He has at Florida Atlantic University an a.m. talk show.

These four impressive young men entered a university setting as "at risk" freshmen. They emerged over a four year period as innovative, successful leaders in different areas of campus life.

### In the fall of 1996 David Gill wrote:

*Seeing myself graduating is definitely... a clear picture. But what I will be doing after that is another. What I do see is myself being known among a huge group of people. I believe I will be very successful, but the road to success will be a difficult one.*

*Today I think that the world is almost made up entirely of problems, most of which are just not necessary; like war: countries battling for power over other countries. Also...diseases that we bring upon ourselves...then there is pollution which we create. But when it affects our society we complain. And then there's racism, and still large amounts of segregation.*

*Four years from now, I don't think anything could get better. It's hard for people to make things right. It's too easy for people to let things go wrong, and society as a whole has become very lazy.*

*In the year 2000 I believe that equality for all races will be my fight. That countries all around the world should come to some peace. The U.S. is a great example of how different societies can work together. So why can't everyone do the same? I mean everyone wants peace. Everyone wants freedom. So then, what's the problem?*

*What I most value is not something specific. I value friendships, present and past. I also value relationships, present and past. I also value relationships, because they make the soul grow. And I value family, that brings unity in a close group.*

*All of my life my learning problems have just gotten in the way of my goals. This year I plan on working on my learning styles to make the best of whatever situation I am in, wherever I am.*

Marsha A. Glines, Ph.D.

*David Gill writes in May 1999:*
*In high school I had the support of my parents and friends to succeed, although I didn't.*

*Not because I couldn't, but because I wouldn't. When I was finally steered in the right direction, my freshman year in college I began to become the person I was actually capable of being. And by believing in myself, here I am.*

David maintains he first became involved at the University because he was nominated by a faculty member in The Advancement Program to become part of a service organization on campus. He believes this was his first step toward involvement and later toward a leadership role in campus life.

**All four campus leaders discussed the support of their families through their academic struggles in school.**

*Ben:*
*Family and friends are first on the list of what I value. I am one of the luckiest students; had lots of family support. They believed in me and pushed me which lead to conflicts but the pushing helped. Mom and Dad did know best! My mom found the high school for me and fought our county to get me into the right school. She struggled for me. The proper choice of a college is important. A support program at a small private college was right for me. Any ADD, dyslexic, or Learning Disabled student can tell you we may not do well in classes of 300 students where you can't be helped individually.*

*I would not have made it without my parents especially during those fragile years of adolescence. I was a brat and always got into trouble.*

*Jason:*
*I value family. I appreciate them for the support I get. For a long time I didn't think my mom believed in me – but it was out of love that she took me to many Learning Disabled doctors, different schools, etc.*

**These four students were asked if they felt they had a solid sense of their learning styles, abilities, potential, etc. If so, how/when did they recognize this?**

*Ben:*
*I learn more from a class then a book so I learned I had to attend classes! I've been told I write well for someone who doesn't read much. I'm sure I've learned to write better...I think I'm creative...word choice is creative, description (like in your head) is creative.*

*Jason:*
*Knowing and accepting are two different things. I didn't accept my learning disabilities until college.*

*Dave Gill:*
*Once I began to find success in understanding my learning abilities, second semester freshman year I understood...but I had to believe I could be a good student. You have to give yourself a chance.*

*Dave Hull:*
*I've always known I had a problem—reversing letters and day-dreaming. I was*

*called stupid in 5^th grade in a classroom by a teacher. I was asked to leave one high school because of poor grades. I never accepted my learning differences until Lynn University.*

*My mother and father believed in me. "I understand" my dad always said.*

*I began to understand when Dr. Glines said, "You must go to tutoring and classes!"*

**When asked about what specific learning disabilities (problems) they struggled with or had overcome the students shared the following:**

***Ben:***

*I still struggle with reading... I've gotten better and sometimes I enjoy it...but I'd rather watch t.v. I'd rather listen to texts on tape. Yet... I'm better through the eye. I don't want to write for a newspaper but I want to continue to be creative, write scripts, commercials. I still struggle to achieve...but for what? I may never be satisfied. I totally have to keep challenging myself.*

***Dave:***

*I always struggle and work on memorizing and making myself do it! I started my freshman year without skills—now I'm fine tuning my reading, trying to read a newspaper daily. I know myself better as a learner now. I know what I have to work on....My weaknesses will always be in math...but I don't like to talk about weakness. In terms of strengths my speaking skills and relationship skills, working with others, delegating are my strengths. I believe leadership positions bring this out – encourages you – but it's the potential...that has always been there. I have learned to repeat everything when I study. I write, type and then say information to myself.*

***Jason:***

*When I was younger I had a grudge against others because it took me longer to process information. In the end, I was better off because success is based on struggle Success is appreciated if it comes after a struggle. There is a sense of accomplishment. When times get tough and it takes a lot of time to complete something – I'm the one who can get it done and put in the effort.*

***Dave Hull:***

*I have long and short term memory problems. I was horrible with core courses— Math and English. My organization skills got me through. My interpersonal skills I've relied on... I learned to use flash cards for everything. "Let your ears hear what your eyes see" is what I learned from tutoring. I now listen and learn.*

**Asked if they had any advice for learning disabled students who are ready to enter college the students replied.**

***Ben:***

*Definitely the fewer students in a class, the more is given. Personal 1 on 1 attention, good tutoring and special programs are a must. We can't be just a face or a number. Having a mentor, someone who guides you—someone you admire who can guide you through problems is important. Confidence is the major issue—anyone who supports you, helps you believe you can be a leader. Its about feeling confidence.*

*Dave:*
*Never give up. Nothing is unrealistic. Anything is possible.*
*Jason:*
*Make sure you know the school – many colleges say they have support but ask the right questions and tour the LD college program on the campus. Talk to other students.*
*Dave Hull:*
*There must be people to help you....like Dr. Glines and The Advancement Program advisors. It's hard to know if there are people there, but meet the people or person running the Learning Disabled Program at the colleges you visit.*

**At what point did you recognize or believe you could be a campus leader?**
*Ben:*
*Everyone has doubts. In my later years of high school I got past the problem that I was always last to finish a test. I began to realize I compensate and may be brighter than some other kids. I went to Lynn University and was apprehensive about being at a 4 year school but the support was here and then I helped myself. To reach down within myself and take risks, make up my mind to do something is easier when support is there. The more support, the easier to trust.*
*Dave:*
*I was given an opportunity (when nominated by a faculty member) to become a campus leader. I still didn't realize all sophomore year whether I could do this until elected chairman of Knights of the Round Table. As chairman I got feedback that was positive about how I was running the organization. I felt supported by Lynn University but you still have to believe in yourself.*
*Jason:*
*There wasn't one point....in time I believed that I could maybe make a difference. I saw things that weren't being done and I took charge. I took a big risk. I was self-conscious...would I do a good job? But, it was a risk I was willing to take. Except for my education this was the first big risk I took.*
*Dave Hull:*
*Leadership...I feel I've always had the ability...that...people listen to me. Opportunity on campus I went after. The main reason I took responsibility for the radio station was I believed I could treat people differently and change the attitude and focus of the station. It needed to be about teaching and fun, not professional radio alone. I work well under pressure.*

Supportive parenting during difficult adolescent years, faculty mentoring and a social environment that provides students the opportunity to understand themselves so they can dare to take appropriate risks and experience leadership and a "take charge" position are all critical components to student success. In an excellent article, "Patterns of Change and Predictors of Success in Individuals with Learning Disabilities: Results From a Twenty-Year Longitudinal Study" written by Marshall H. Raskind, Roberta J. Goldberg, Eleanor L.Higgins and Kenneth L. Herman, (Learning Disabilities Research and Practice, 1999) a quantitative analysis is presented. This analysis suggests that the success of their particular study group of learning disabled individuals may be related to "(a) realistic adaptation to life events including greater self-awareness/self-acceptance of the learning disability, pro-activity, perseverance and emotional stability; (b) goal setting; (c) presence and use of effective support systems."

In addition to these identified "success attributes," the authors, again citing research conducted at the Frostig Center, concluded that individuals with learning disabilities tended to be "late bloomers."

So, this is our audience. The challenge continues to be how to embrace these non-traditional late bloomers, these learning disabled students, to trust and believe in themselves, take risks and ultimately emerge as our future leaders.

Adapted from the anticipated publication of
Past Reflections, Present Realities, Future Aspirations:
Non-traditional Students As Leaders in the New Millennium

by Marsha A. Glines

# Chapter Eight

# Building a Team for College: Collaborative Advocacy

*Frank Kline, Ph.D.*
Associate Professor and Assistant Dean for Teacher Education
Seattle Pacific University

After some basic background information on the differences between the services available in high school and those available in college, this chapter focuses on how services for students with learning disabilities can be obtained/provided in a collaborative fashion through a process of advocacy. Suggestions are provided for college students and parents in terms of working with educational service communities within colleges to obtain high quality educational services for students with learning disabilities.

### Differences Between College and High School Services

Services for students with learning disabilities at the college level differ significantly from services at the high school level. The difference is due to differences in the laws covering students with disabilities at the various levels. The Individuals with Disabilities Education Act (IDEA) covers students at the high school level. This act actually guarantees services for students from the ages of 3 until they are 21 or until they graduate from high school whichever comes first. Section 504 of the Rehabilitation Act of 1973 (504) covers any person with a disability who works for agencies who get federal funds. The Americans with Disabilities Act (ADA) covers employment by a business, public services and accommodations, telecommunications, and various miscellaneous issues. Thus, while 504 and ADA cover students while they are in both high school and college, IDEA does not cover students in college.

While there isn't room for an exhaustive contrast and comparison of the various laws here, there are at least three salient differences that need to be highlighted in a discussion of services for students in college. First, the definition of disability, second, the requirement for services to the institution, and third, how decisions are made.

In order to be identified as eligible for services under IDEA, students must fall within one or more of thirteen categories of disability. Not only must a student qualify within a category, but they must also need special education because of the disability. The thirteen categories are; mentally retarded, hearing impaired, speech or language impaired, seriously emotionally disturbed, visually impaired, other health impaired, deaf, deaf-blind, multiply disabled, specific learning disabilities, autistic, or traumatic brain injured. The criteria for inclusion in each category are often quite complex. In addition to meeting the categorical requirements, the person must need the services. Just being disabled isn't sufficient. In order to qualify under IDEA, students must also need special education and/or related services. Eligibility is crucial not only for the student, but also for the district. It is through the count of students qualifying for services that the district is reimbursed for part of the services provided.

Eligibility for services under both 504 and ADA is quite different. Neither law provides any reimbursement for services provided. Both are civil rights laws guaranteeing for persons with disabilities the same rights and responsibilities that other people have. For that reason, the eligibility requirements are very different from those under IDEA. 504 requires only that persons must have a physical or mental impairment which substantially limits a major life activity, have a record of such an impairment, or are regarded as having such an impairment. Major life activities include walking, seeing, hearing, speaking, breathing, learning, working, caring for oneself, and performing manual tasks. As you can see, 504 covers a much broader group of people than IDEA; it is not limited by age and its criteria for eligibility are much less stringent and complex. ADA and 504 are very similar in their definition and eligibility requirements. Any student covered by IDEA would also be covered by 504 and ADA. However, there are students not covered by IDEA who could possibly be covered by 504 and ADA.

The second difference that we shall examine is in the institution's requirements to serve students. IDEA actually reimburses schools for a percentage of expenses associated with services provided. What's more, IDEA requires districts to go out and find students with disabilities. This "child find" requirement is built into IDEA. Each district is required to actively search for students having disabilities in the area they serve. Because of the reimbursement involved and the "child find" requirements in the law, it is very much in the interest of the schools to actively search and identify as many students as possible to receive special education services.

504 and ADA on the other hand, are civil rights laws. There are no rewards for providing services under 504 and ADA, but there can be very large penalties for not providing required services. Neither 504 nor ADA require institutions to actively seek students with disabilities. Institutions are required to provide services, but they are not required to actively search for persons with disabilities to serve. Since institutions are required to provide services but are not reimbursed for any services provided, and because there is no "child find" provision in the law, it is not necessarily in the interest of institutions to identify students as needing services. This is the reason that self-advocacy is so important at the college level. To receive services, students must step forward and identify themselves as being disabled.

Finally, there are differences in how services are provided to persons having disabilities under IDEA and 504 or ADA. Under IDEA, a multidisciplinary team (MDT) is formed by the schools and charged with the responsibility of determining eligibility and the services necessary for each person with disabilities. Parents, and when appropriate the student, are mandated members of the MDT. It is the MDT that makes the key decisions about the kind of services students with disabilities will receive. These services are specified in an Individualized Educational Plan (IEP).

Under 504, there is no requirement for an MDT. There is a requirement that decisions be made by a group of persons knowledgeable about the child, the evaluation information considered, and the service options available. While an IEP is not required, institutions are required to have an appropriate "plan" listing the accommodations provided. Most institutions use a group of persons knowledgeable about the student to specify the plan.

### Collaborative Relationships

Collaborative relationships are quite different at high school and college. In high school under the IDEA, schools must convene an MDT to determine eligibility and services. That team, by law, includes parents and also students where appropriate. That means that collaborative relationships between home and school are actually legally mandated. While 504 specifies that groups of people work together on specifying the plan, there are no requirements that the student's family be included. This makes for a very different relationship between the institution and the person with disabilities. Before we begin to explore various models of relationship, let's consider what collaboration itself is.

### Collaboration

Collaboration indicates a team approach and a substantial degree of communication, but it also allows and even requires the participating professions and communities to be different in some way. Knackendoffel, & Robinson, (1992) define collaboration as an ongoing process whereby persons with different expertise voluntarily work together to create solutions to problems that are impeding a student's success, as well as, to carefully monitor and refine those solutions. Two or more individuals working for a common goal, mutual benefits, or desired outcomes characterize collaboration.

Knackendoffel & Robinson (1992) highlighted a few beliefs that must be central to a collaborative relationship. Those involved in collaborative relationships must believe that all participants can contribute to the process, all participants have something to learn about working with children, that services offered for children improve as interested parties work together rather than in isolation. Collaboration is enhanced by trust, respect, openness, and clear communication among participants. As collaboration occurs, participants will learn to work in new ways and acquire new skills. These beliefs are key to the most effective forms of collaboration.

### Legal requirements for collaboration in high school settings

In 1975 Congress passed Public Law 94-142. A primary purpose of passing this law was to assure that children with disabilities have available to them free and appropriate education that emphasizes special education and related services designed to meet their unique needs. 'Special education' is a set of services provided to meet the unique needs of a student in special education (OSPI, 1999). "Related services are those services required by a student to allow them to benefit from their special education program" (p.16). The court case of *Irving Independent School District vs. Tatro* affirms that it is the schools responsibility to provide support services allowing meaningful access to education for a child with a disability. This law promotes and requires the collaboration and joint efforts of schoolteachers and parents in the education of children.

The formation of an Individualized Education Plan (IEP) for children who receive special education services is the mechanism through which the law promotes collaboration. Turnbull (1993) described the IEP as a method for assessing the child based on nondiscriminatory evaluation for purposes of prescribing an appropriate educational program. The evaluation is an ongoing process and therefore, ongoing communication must occur within the IEP team.

### Legal requirements for collaboration in post-secondary settings.

As mentioned above, students having disabilities in post-secondary settings including colleges and universities are not without protection. Section 504 and the ADA provide protection against an "otherwise qualified" person being discriminated against on the basis of his/her disability. An obvious example is of a person required by disability to use a wheelchair. That person cannot be excluded from a class simply because there is no physical access to the room for the wheelchair. Less obviously, but perhaps more germane to this audience, a person who reads poorly cannot be discriminated against in classes which do not include reading as part of their objectives. Therefore, in a geography class, a student who is otherwise qualified for the class but who cannot read must be provided with alternative means of access to information commonly obtained through the written word. That may include accommodations such as books on tapes for the text, a reader for various tests, and other kinds of accommodations which allow the student to gain, through various other methods, the information that is normally acquired by reading.

Under IDEA, these kinds of accommodations would be specified within the IEP. Under 504 and ADA, there is no IEP, but there is a "plan." The plan is developed by a group of individuals familiar with the individual and the disability. While there is no requirement that parents or even the student be included in the group, it makes sense that they would be. After all, who is better acquainted with an individual and their needs than persons close to them who have observed them across years of schooling and the individual themselves. There are however, significant barriers to the inclusion of such people in the group.

### Barriers to Collaboration

Barriers to collaboration can be broken into two types: those barriers within parents and students, and those barriers within the institution. We will consider each in turn.

*Barriers within parents and students*

Students and parents who have probably lived with the disability in question for many years by the time a person is ready for college, undoubtedly have the most complete and specific knowledge about the unique situation. However, their very closeness to the situation inevitably includes a certain bias. That bias can be expressed as an attitude and certain attitudes are less conducive to good collaborative relationships than others. Specific attitudes that can damage collaborative relationships are defensiveness and an inability to focus on the specific situation at hand.

Defensiveness can take many forms. It can include denial of a problem, a certain guilt about a disability or a feeling of responsibility for the disability. However it manifests itself, it includes as part of its distinguishing characteristics, a desire to justify oneself. This can occur through an attempt to apportion blame to others, it can be a series of attempts to excuse behavior, or it can occur through an attempt to place inordinate value on the efforts that one has made. Whatever the manifestation, defensiveness does not lead to a productive collaborative relationship. The focus is more on what could have, should have, or was done rather than on what might be, or will be, done.

Another attitude that can lead to poor collaborative relationships is an inability to focus on the current situation. Certainly the past can be helpful in understanding how a situation developed. However, it can also be a smoke screen allowing one to escape from the current reality. When focusing on the past is used in the latter sense, it doesn't build collaborative relationships, but rather damages them. The person who can't seem to focus on the situation at hand and continually harkens back to other situations less relevant is seen as obstructing a healthy solution.

Another barrier to good collaboration is a lack of information. This may seem ironic since families have more information than anyone else about a particular disability. However, it is not uncommon for that information to be less accessible than would be helpful. There are at least two kinds of records that should be kept and shared. First, school records. Each student served under IDEA is provided with an IEP. Each IEP includes several parts detailing the kinds of special education services that were provided. This information is very helpful for people trying to establish a 504 plan. IEPs can also be used to establish a disability for purposes of eligibility under 504 or ADA.

Other records that can be useful include transcripts, attendance records, grades, discipline records, any notes from teachers, protocols from various tests, old copies of IEPs, various projects that have been saved, etc. The school will save some of these records at least for a short time after graduation. Families and students are entitled to a copy of the records should they need or ask for them. However, it is good to make the request and to obtain a copy shortly before graduation time. Records are purged on a regular basis and may be unavailable thus losing important and helpful information about a student. Very possibly, a family or student will not desire to share all information in the school record. However, if they have the information, they can choose to share parts that are relevant and not share information that is less relevant.

Other records that can be useful include medical records. Doctors go to great lengths to maintain accurate records of each contact with a patient. These contacts often involve information about disabilities that can impact learning and suggest accommodations. For that reason, they should be available for selection and sharing. As with school records, a family or student may choose to not share all of the information in the records. If they have copies of the records, they can be perused and appropriate, important information shared. If the records are not available, of course there is no option of sharing them.

The final barrier to good collaboration is poor communication skills. Humans communicate with various degrees of effectiveness. Certainly, many disabilities themselves include impaired communication as part of their manifestations. For whatever reason, poor communication skills can be a barrier to effective collaboration. There are at least two communication skills that are critical to good collaboration—listening, and the ability to understand a problem fully before jumping to solutions.

Listening is critical to any form of communication. Collaboration can be conceived as communication to address a problem. If communication doesn't occur, there can be no collaboration. The most critical of communication skills for collaboration are receptive rather than expressive. Listening and reading are very important in collaborative efforts. Listening can be enhanced by a realization of how important it is to listen. It can also be enhanced by a careful paraphrase of what you hear a person to say. That allows them to correct any misunderstandings that may have occurred. As one listens, it is important to listen for more than the content. By listening to the feeling tone as well as the content, one can gather more information about the topic being discussed and discern the person's attitude toward the topic.

Another communication deficit that can create a barrier is to focus too quickly on a solution. Often, delaying a discussion of actual accommodations until the nature of the disability and the tasks at hand are clearly presented can be very beneficial. If a person identifies a solution too quickly, it is easy to end up fighting for a particular solution rather than to deal effectively with the problem. Often problems have more than one solution. While various solutions may be equally effective in terms of addressing a problem they may not be equally attractive to one or more of the parties involved. For that reason alone, it is important not to commit to one solution too quickly. Waiting until the problem is carefully delimited and even until several potential solutions may be shared will strengthen the final outcome considerably.

*Barriers within institutions*

Several barriers to collaboration along with potential solutions to these barriers have been identified from the perspective of a family and/or person with a disability. There are other barriers related more to the agencies involved. These barriers can also be overcome. One of the key barriers is training in collaborative skills. Skrtic and Sailor (1997) suggested that professionals involved in system transformation must have specialized skills in collaboration, and inter professional information sharing and language systems. They stated that agencies should have a consumer database that is shared, as well as confidentiality waiver forms. The services should be family focused and community managed (Skrtic & Sailor, 1997).

Related to training in collaborative skills is a service orientation. Some institutions seem to have their own preservation more at heart than service to their customers. While the economic model holds grave dangers for education, the idea of service doesn't. Educators need to have the best interests of their clients in mind and need to pursue them assiduously. Unfortunately, many do not. This barrier is analogous to an attitude barrier in a family and is manifested by lack of attention, poor responsiveness to requests, overly rigid adherence to policies, etc.

The most prominent suggestions for overcoming barriers of this nature are creating a shared vision among all of the people, creating a clearly defined system with clear roles and administrative support, and increasing the professionals' knowledge of what the other systems can offer to the child and the family.

While the ultimate responsibility for institutional collaboration resides with the institution, parents can help promote collaboration. Harvey (1995) noted that family involvement is critical in developing a system of care. Five guiding ideas for families to remember in order to help facilitate effective collaboration follow: choose your institution carefully, suggest collaboration, share information among various parts of the institution, facilitate scheduling and take a proactive role in developing appropriate services.

1. Parents want the best care for their children. Carefully picking a post-secondary institution with a good reputation for services to students with disabilities and who

collaborate increases the chances of this.  One of the other chapters in this book provides good direction in selecting an appropriate college.

2.  Parents can suggest collaboration to institutions of higher education.  After making this suggestion a parent must make sure that they are available and that appropriate release forms for other potential collaborators such as physicians and educators are on file.

3.  Families and students with disabilities can initiate communication about disabilities.  In fact, at the post secondary level, if parents or students do not initiate communication about disabilities, no services will be provided!  Only when a disability is brought to the attention of the institution are accommodations required.

4.  Schedules are a major part of any school.  Devising an appropriate schedule is difficult at best and nearly impossible at colleges.  Advising is difficult.  It is important that the family and the student know as much about the schedule and advisement issues as possible and that they be proactive in seeking help in these issues.  By knowing the schedules and requirements of programs of interest, a parent can help arrange necessary classes and schedules.

5.  Parents can also help to initiate appropriate interagency collaboration between post-secondary institutions and other agencies important to their children with disabilities.  Facilitating appropriate record sharing between high schools, medical communities and institutions of higher education can be very beneficial to students with disabilities.  While it takes time and energy, parents can be catalysts to build the necessary relationships for collaboration and help start various models of interagency collaboration.

**Models of Collaboration**

There are various models of collaborative efforts in post-secondary institutions.  Some of them involve working with other agencies, others within various agencies, and yet others collaborative efforts with clients and/or families of clients.  We will explore these latter models here.  The basic model of collaboration under IDEA will be described as a contrast.  A non-collaborative and then a collaborative model for services under 504 and ADA will be described.

*Models Under I.D.E.A.*

Under IDEA, collaboration is mandated.  That is, through the multidisciplinary team, various professionals are required to collaborate with parents.  Parents must be included on the team as eligibility and various types of services are decided.  The basic process is that each professional involved accomplishes their evaluation and formulates recommendations relative to their area of expertise independently.  Those observations are then pooled in a meeting, often called a staffing.  At the staffing the various pertinent decisions are made with each attendant having an important role and the ability to share their information and voice their concerns.

This model of collaboration varies in its effectiveness depending upon the collaborative skills of the individuals involved as well as the policies of the school.  However, the basic outline of the process is mandated and consistent across districts.

*Models Under 504 and A.D.A.*

As noted above, there is no requirement for parent/family participation in decisions regarding 504 or ADA. That means that the agencies themselves are largely responsible for making relevant decisions about the kinds of services that are offered. Two models of how those decisions are made are provided below.

### Traditional Model

Traditionally, students and families of students with disabilities are minimally included in the decisions made about accommodations. The process starts when a student identifies him or her self as disabled to the 504 officer. Once that declaration has been made, the officer asks for any documents that confirm and describe the disability. Once the eligibility for services has been determined, the nature of the services is determined. This often involves the student or the family minimally as sources of information. The accommodations are determined, shared with professors who have the student in class and the student then is on their own.

### Advocacy Model

An alternative model that is more collaborative is based on student advocacy. If pursued with an appropriate attitude, advocacy doesn't need to involve an adversarial relationship. The suggested advocacy is based on a process similar to that used in development of an IEP with the students themselves in charge of the process. It forms a cycle of assessment, goal setting, strategies to achieve the goals, and monitoring of achievement.

### Assessment

In this case, assessment means an honest self-evaluation of skills in relationship to the tasks at hand. The first step in this process is to evaluate the task at hand. That is, the student should look at the requirements of each course asking questions about the amount of reading, writing, and other tasks that are required. Sources of information about the task can include other students who have taken the course, the course syllabus, the instructor, and the educational services office of the college. This is a place where collaboration with the 504 officer is crucial. They can provide information about each course that will be very helpful.

Once a clear description of the task at hand has been made, the student should evaluate their own skills in relationship to those tasks. The student's self evaluation should be honest and take into account information that he or she may have from former school or work experiences that can inform their ability to achieve the tasks required by each course.

### Goal Setting

Once the assessment process is complete, the student should set goals for each course. These goals take several forms. First of all, they are an overall level of perfor-mance that will be acceptable. Second, they include scheduling information about the work that needs to be accomplished. Third, they include advocacy goals for necessary accommodations.

Specifying an overall level of performance can be helpful. By choosing an overall level of acceptable performance to pursue, the student commits himself or herself to invest in the necessary work to achieve that grade. This goal setting should also be approached in a strategic manner. Not all courses are equally important in terms of the student's life goals. Courses that are more important should receive more attention than those that are less important.

Scheduling goals are critical. Most students are ill equipped for this type of goal setting and yet it can be the most important. Most educational service offices can assist in this process if a student needs help. The process includes mapping of all due dates for projects from each class onto a calendar. Once that map is complete, then self-imposed intermediate due dates are built into the calendar. These include dates for library work for papers, outlines and rough drafts of papers, study goals for tests, and intermediary dates for various kinds of projects. The 504 officer can assist in helping the student do a task analysis for each task and in setting reasonable goals.

By breaking down each larger project into smaller parts, and mapping all projects and smaller parts onto a calendar, the student can better monitor their achievement. This process, if carried out carefully, will build a certain level of accountability within the student. By looking at the over-all map of activities, the student can tell if they are on target to achieve their goal or not.

### Advocacy for Accommodations

Once assessment and goal setting have been achieved, the student is in a strong position to advocate for necessary accommodations. By comparing the self-assessment information with the course-assessment information, a student can request accommodations necessary to meet the demands of the course. These accommodations must be related to the documented disability, and must not be the actual goal of the class. The key to requesting an accommodation is to demonstrate that the need is a result of the disability and that while it is part of the class, it is not the objective of the class. The student must demonstrate that they are "otherwise qualified" and would suffer discrimination without the accommodation. Hopefully, this will also be a collaborative process as the college represented by the 504 officer, helps to identify resources that are available to help the student meet their needs.

### Monitoring

The final step of the advocacy cycle is to monitor progress. Using the detailed set of goals specified near the beginning of the cycle, a student can monitor their progress toward the goals that were set. Again, the 504 officer can be helpful here. By setting up regular checkpoints in relationship to class activities and self-imposed goals, the 504 officer can assist in monitoring progress.

### Summary

The focus of this chapter has been on how collaborative relationships differ between high school and college settings. These differences are in part due to the differences in laws governing the inclusion of students with disabilities. The IDEA governs how schools treat students with disabilities during the years from 3 until high school graduation. Section 504 and the ADA govern how schools, among other institutions, treat students with disabilities in colleges.

One of the basic differences is how disabilities are defined. To be eligible for services under IDEA, one must fit within the definitions of specific categories of disability and must also need special education services. To qualify for accommodations under 504 and ADA, one must have a disability which limits a significant life activity, have had such a disability or be known as disabled to that extent. Thus, students who qualify for services under IDEA also qualify under 504 and ADA. However, not all students who would qualify under 504 or ADA would qualify under IDEA.

In addition to how students are determined to be eligible for services, the laws also differ in terms of how services are provided. IDEA requires that particular people including the parents and the student where appropriate be involved in determining the services provided. There is no such provision for student and family inclusion in 504 or ADA.

In addition, schools are required to search for students who need services under IDEA. However, students who need services under 504 and ADA are required to declare themselves to the institution. The institution has no requirement to search for people with disabilities.

Because institutions have no responsibility to include families or search for people with disabilities under 504 and ADA, obtaining services requires that people with disabilities be proactive in their self-advocacy. Ironically, it is through this proactivity that collaboration can occur. Students and families can select schools with an eye toward the services they provide, make known their desires to collaborate, initiate communication about disabilities, keep track of schedules and advisement, and initiate appropriate interagency collaboration. Students and families can also work toward good goal setting, assess their own knowledge and skills as well as those required for specific classes, suggest specific accommodations that might be helpful, and monitor progress. These kinds of activities will help build a productive and collaborative team to help students with learning disabilities in a college setting.

# Chapter Nine

# Creating Options: A Resource on Financial Aid for Students With Disabilities

*Reprinted with permission of HEATH Resource Center*

March 2000. Updated by Daniel Gardner from material prepared previously by HEATH. Careful review and comments by Susan Luhman of the National Association of Student Financial Aid Administrators and Polly Huston of the Maryland State Department of Education, Division of Rehabilitation Services, were gratefully appreciated.

While education beyond high school in the United States is optional, it has become a necessary investment in future employment and life satisfaction for many people, Most, however, cannot afford to make this investment without some outside monetary assistance. Over the years, public and private sources of money have been developed specifically to meet this need. As increasing, but limited, amounts of money have become available, a standardized method of determining eligibility has evolved to promote equitable distribution of student financial aid.

Financial aid is based on a partnership among the student, parents, postsecondary educational institutions, state and federal governments, and available private resources. For the student with a disability, the partnership also may include a Vocational Rehabilitation agency and the Social Security Administration. Such a partnership requires cooperation from all and an understanding by each of their responsibilities within the financial aid process.

Obtaining financial aid can be a complex process. Laws frequently are amended, and eligibility requirements, policy, and disbursement of governmental funds change each year. As the costs of a postsecondary education rise, keeping informed about changes in the financial aid system becomes imperative.

This resource paper provides an overview of student financial aid and discusses the roles and responsibilities of those who play a significant part in the process of providing aid to students with disabilities. The paper also addresses the financial aid application procedure and suggests timelines and resources for these individuals who are seeking financial aid. The information in this paper was based on the best available information at the time of publication in March 2000 and reflects information for the 2000-2001 school year. The HEATH staff have prepared this resource paper for students, parents, and all professionals who assist students with disabilities in securing financial assistance for postsecondary education.

The discussion below covers the various types of financial aid, the technical words and phrases used to describe them, and the process involved in their disbursement. Particular attention is given to those expenses that are considered disability-related, and suggestions are made about ways in which some of those expenses may be met. Also included is a brief description of Vocational Rehabilitation (VR) Agencies, the services that they may provide, and the interaction between the state VR agency and the financial aid office of a postsecondary institution. Finally, suggestions are offered about additional possibilities for financial assistance.

**What Is Financial Aid?**

Financial aid is designed to help individuals meet their educational expenses when their own resources are not sufficient. A student who believes that his or her own and family resources are not sufficient to pay for all the costs of attendance (tuition, room and board, books, transportation, campus activities, etc.) should apply for financial aid through the financial aid office of the institution he or she plans to attend.

Four types of aid are available:

1. Grants—Aid that generally does not have to be repaid.

2. Loans—Money borrowed to cover school costs, which must be repaid (usually with interest) over a specified period of time (usually after the student has left school or graduated).
3. Work-study—Employment that enables a student to earn money toward a portion of school costs during or between periods of enrollment.
4. Scholarships—Gifts and awards based on a student's academic achievement, background, or other criteria.

**Federal Financial Aid**

The federal government contributes to the first three types of student financial aid. These programs are explained in a booklet called *Funding Your Education* from the U.S. Department of Education. For a free copy, write to Federal Student Aid Programs, Box 84, Washington, DC 20044 or call (800) 433-3243 or (800) 730-8913 (TTY). The booklet is also available at the following Web address: http://www.ed.gov/prog info/SFA/FYE/.

The programs described in the booklet are:
1. Federal Pell Grants
2. Federal Supplemental Educational Opportunity Grants (FSEOG)
3. Federal Work-Study (FWS)
4. Federal Perkins Loans
5. Federal Family Education Loans (FFEL) including:
   a. Federal Stafford Loans (subsidized and unsubsidized)
   b. Federal PLUS Loans
6. William D. Ford Direct Loans including:
   a. Federal Direct Loans (subsidized and unsubsidized)
   b. Federal Direct PLUS Loans

All of these programs, except the unsubsidized and PLUS loans, are based on the financial need of the student and his or her family. Although the PLUS and unsubsidized loan programs do not take into account any family contribution, these loans (individually or combined) cannot exceed the difference between the student's cost of attending a postsecondary institution and the student's other financial aid (including scholarships).

Generally, a postsecondary school participates in either the Federal Family Education Loan Program or the Direct Loan Program. A student may not borrow both a Federal Stafford and Direct PLUS simultaneously for the same student. The terms and conditions of the Direct Loan programs mirror those of the FEEL programs, except that the Direct Loan programs carry additional repayment options.

Financial assistance is also available through AmeriCorps, a program authorized under the National and Community Service Trust Act of 1993.

This program provides individuals ages 17 and over with the opportunity to earn education awards of $4,725 in exchange for full-time service of at least one year or part-time service of at least two years in an approved program of community service. An individual may serve up to two terms and earn up to two education awards. For more information about exchanging national or community service for educational funding, contact AmeriCorps at (800) 942-2677 or visit their web site: http://www.cns.gov/americorps/.

Some colleges, states, and other entities may also offer aid that is merit-based, which means that funds are provided to students without regard to financial need if certain conditions (such as high grades) are met. The financial aid administrator at the school of your choice is the best resource for locating merit-based or any other financial aid resources for attending that school.

### What Application Do I Complete?

All students applying for federal assistance are required to complete the Free Application for Federal Student Aid (FAFSA). Students who applied for federal financial aid in the previous year have the option of completing a Renewal Free Application for Federal Student Aid (Renewal FAFSA). There is no charge to complete or process the FAFSA or the Renewal FAFSA.

The Department of Education develops the FAFSA and the Renewal FAFSA in both paper and electronic formats. To apply, students may use any of the following formats:

- FAFSA of the Web
- FAFSA Express software
- EDExpress application software
- The paper FAFSA

---

**FINANCIAL NEED**

**Educational Expenses**
Tuition, fees, books and supplies, personal computers, room, board, transportation, personal expenses, dependent care, expenses related to disability, study abroad costs, cooperative education costs. *

**Family Contribution**
Amount family and/or student is expected to contribute toward cost of education (contribution from income or assets, social security benefits, welfare, etc.)

**Financial Need**
May be met by financial aid package. (See subheading "What Is a Financial Aid Package?" on page109)

*Some expenses may not be considered in the determination of financial need. (See subheading "What Expenses Are Considered Disability Related?" on page 111)

---

FAFSA on the Web allows students to complete a FAFSA online and submit it via the Internet. To learn more about this process, visit the following web site: http://www.fafsa.ed.gov.

FAFSA Express is a software program that allows students to apply for federal student aid from their home computer. Students can order a copy on diskette by calling 1-800-801-0576 or download the program from the U.S. Department of Education's web site at http://www.ed.gov/offices/OFSAP/Students/apply/fexpress.html. Students who do not have a home computer can use this program at a public library, college or high school that has a copy of FAFSA Express for public use.

Some schools will complete the application for students using an electronic software product developed for use by schools only called EDExpress. Students must first check with their school to make sure that it has EDExpress application capability.

**What is the Family Contribution?**

The family contribution is the amount of money the family of a student is expected to contribute toward college expenses. The family includes the student and the student's parents in the case of a dependent student, or the student (and spouse, if any) in the case of an independent student. The amount the family is expected to contribute is calculated by a standardized formula that takes into account the family's financial resources (income and assets), family size, and basic living expenses. The calculation of family contribution is based on information provided by the student's family on a standardized need analysis form.

Before completing the FAFSA, students must first determine their dependency status. If, for the purposes of applying for financial aid, the student is considered to be dependent, then the student and the student's parents must complete the FAFSA.

If the student is considered to be independent, only the student (and the student's spouse, if married) must complete the FAFSA. A student may qualify as financially independent if he or she is: 24 years of age or older by December 31 of the award year (12/31/00 for the 2000-2001 award year), is a veteran of the armed forces of the United States, will be a graduate or professional student for 2000-2001, is an orphan or ward of the court, is married, has legal dependents other than a spouse, or is a student for whom a financial aid administrator makes a documented determination of independence by reason of other unusual circumstances.

Students who are also applying for non-federal financial assistance from postsecondary institutions or from their state of residence may be required to complete an additional form, and may be required to pay a fee for processing this information. Check with the financial aid offices of the colleges or universities that your are interested in attending to determine what additional forms for non-federal assistance you should file.

The financial aid office can also tell you about the availability of state aid and whether you will need to file an additional form to apply for such aid. The financial aid office can either supply you with any additional forms needed to apply for state aid or tell you how to obtain the necessary forms. If you reside in a state other than the one in which the college is located, the college can tell you where to obtain this information for the state in which you reside.

### What is the cost of Attendance?

Each college or university must estimate the costs a student will reasonably encounter in order to attend that institution. Cost of attendance will always include a figure for tuition and fees. Supplies needed for course work are sometimes included in tuition, but more often books and supplies are estimated separately. Cost of attendance should also include estimates for living expenses—primarily room and board, but also a moderate amount for personal and miscellaneous expenses. Cost of attendance is sometimes called "cost of education" or student budget."

For students living in dormitories or other local housing, cost of attendance estimates should include transportation for trips between the student's home and the college or university at the beginning and end of the period of attendance, as well as any breaks during which the institution closes its housing facilities. For a student commuting daily from home, transportation includes a reasonable amount for commuting, usually using public transportation if it is available. Purchase of a car for commuting purposes may not be considered an education-related expense, although the basic maintenance of a car during the student's enrollment may be included. Also, new rules allow students to include the cost of purchasing or renting a personal computer in the cost of attendance.

In addition, costs related to a student's particular personal circumstances may also be included if they are incurred as a result of attending the college or university. For example, cost of attendance may include day-care costs for students with dependent children. Expenses associated with a period of study abroad that is part of the student's educational program, or during a cooperative education experience, may also increase a student's cost of attendance. Costs related to a student's disability may also be included under certain circumstances (see page 111).

A student who believes his or her costs are higher than the standard estimated by the college or university should ask to speak with the institution's financial aid administrator.

Whether a student is taking classes on a full-time or part-time basis may also impact his or her cost of attendance. A student's "enrollment status" is usually measured as full time, three-quarter time, half time, or less than half time. The definition of these measurements may vary at different institutions but federal rules establish certain minimum definitions that must be used when determining the amount of a student's federal financial aid. Although a college or university may increase the amount of work required to classify a student as full time, an institution may not reduce the federal minimum definition for any reason. However, a college or university may allow a student with unusual circumstances (such as a disability) extra time to complete his or her program and may award financial aid during the extra terms of periods of enrollment.

The amount of tuition estimated for a student attending on a part-time basis is generally less than the amount estimated for full time attendance. The allowances for books and travel might also be less for a part-time student. Allowances for room and board and certain other costs are eliminated entirely for students who attend less than half time. In addition to affecting a student's cost of attendance, part-time enrollment directly affects the maximum amount allowable under certain aid programs.

**What is Financial Need?**

The financial need of a student is the difference between the student's educational expenses and the amount of money the family is expected to contribute. In general terms, the formula to determine financial need is shown in the box on page 106.

There is no guarantee, however, that any one institution will be able to meet the total financial need of any given student.

**What is the financial aid process?**

The financial aid process is designed to equitably serve the approximately 19.5 million undergraduate and graduate students currently enrolled at more than 7,000 postsecondary educational institutions. The scope of the financial aid system requires that the application process be standardized. Describing special circumstances or needs, therefore, may require additional effort on the part of the applicant. Applicants who have special needs, such as disability-related expenses, should express those needs to the aid administrator at the postsecondary institution. Because of the complexity of the system, however, they must take care to express those needs within the context of the system as explained below.

According to many directors of financial aid, taking care to be early and accurate in applying for aid is the most important step in the financial aid process. However, completing the financial aid application form early requires you to report income tax information well in advance of the April 15th Internal Revenue Service (IRS) tax filing deadline. Campus financial aid administrators suggest that a family complete the tax information in time to file the FAFSA (and any additional non-federal forms) by the college's or university's deadline, or use an estimate rather than delay completing and processing the form. A processed application can be corrected if the actual IRS tax information differs from the estimate. If an individual's processed aid application is not received by the date specified by the college or university, the student may lose priority for many forms of aid, both federal and institutional. Students and their families should be aware that because aid application deadlines vary from institution to institution and may call for differing information, early preparation will ensure that all deadlines can be met with appropriate information. If the college or university requests documentation of application information, such as signed tax returns or verification statements, the family must comply by the deadlines for those documents to keep the aid application process on track.

It is also important to note that students must reapply for financial aid every year.

**What is a Financial Aid Package?**

A financial aid package is a combination of financial aid resources (grants, loans, work-study) put together by the institution's financial aid administrator and designed to meet, as closely as possible, a student's individual financial need. The amount and types of assistance in a package depend on the cost of attendance at a particular institution, the student's need, availability of funds at the institution, and funds available from outside sources. Thus, a student may be offered two different financial aid packages if he or she applies to two different institutions. Students should compare not only the dollars offered, but also the composition of the financial aid package from each institution. The following examples illustrate different packages of financial aid that a student might be offered at two different institutions. School A costs $5,000 to attend, and School B costs $10,000. (See box below.)

Note: The aid amounts are for illustration purposes only and do not necessarily reflect actual amounts a student could expect from a similar school.

In the examples below, School B offers $8,600 this year, whereas School A offers less than half that. However, if the student chooses School B, he or she must find $400 more than the expected family contribution. On the other hand, School B may have the academic program of choice and the necessary support services. Thus, the student may believe that in the long run, School B is the right choice.

In addition to comparing the total dollars offered in aid by each institution, however, students need to consider level of indebtedness, terms of loan repayment, and the institution's policy on how the aid packages will be constructed in subsequent years. Students, their families, financial aid personnel, and where relevant, rehabilitation counselors of students with disabilities should evaluate the amount of debt a student

|  | School A | School B |
|---|---|---|
| **COST OF ATTENDANCE** | $5,000 | $10,000 |
| **FAMILY CONTRIBUTION** | $1,000 | $9,000 |
| **Need for Financial Aid** (cost minus family contribution) | $4,000 | $9,000 |
| **SOURCES OF FINANCIAL AID** | | |
| Federal Pell Grant | $1,100 | $1,100 |
| Federal Campus-based Aid (FSEOG, Work-Study, Perkins) | $1,500 | $3,000 |
| Aid from Institution | $400 | $2,000 |
| Federal Stafford Loan | $1,000 | $2,500 |
| **Total Financial Aid** | $4,000 | $8,600 |
| **Total Unmet Financial Need** (to be met from outside sources, such as: additional family contribution, PLUS Loans, private employment, Local/disability-specific scholarships, etc.) | $0 | $400 |

can reasonably repay after graduating. Career choices often determine (or are determined by) a student's level of indebtedness and terms of repayment of financial aid loans.

From year to year, financial aid administrators may vary the combination of grant, loan, and work-study money in a student's aid package, emphasizing loans for freshmen and work-study or scholarships in later years—or the other way around. Institutions might not have uniform policies on financial aid package combinations over time. Ask the financial aid administrator what the institution's policy is beyond the first year of study.

**What expenses are considered disability related?**

The student with a disability is often faced with additional expenses not incurred by other students. These may include:

- Special equipment (related to the disability) and its maintenance.
- Cost of services for personal use or study, such as readers, interpreters, note takers, or personal care attendants.
- Transportation, if traditional means are not accessible.
- Medical expenses not covered by insurance that relate directly to the individual's disability.

Students should be sure to inform the aid administrator of disability-related expenses that may previously have been covered by the family budget. These may include food and veterinary bills for guide dogs, batteries for hearing aids and a Typed Text (TTY) [previously called a Telecommunication Device for the Deaf (TDD)], or the cost of recruiting and training readers or personal care attendants.

Leaving home often necessitates the purchase of new or additional equipment that will allow the student to be independent at college. For example, the student's secondary school may have furnished an adapted computer or other disability-related equipment, but that equipment belongs to and remains at the high school after the student graduates. Students with disabilities should seek assistance from the Office of Disability Support Services and/or the Financial Aid Office to determine disability-related expenses.

Once these expenses have been identified, students should provide the financial aid administrator with documentation of any disability-related expense that is necessary to ensure attainment of the student's educational goal. Where applicable, this documentaiton should also state the amounts that will be covered by insurance and other assisting agencies. Depending on the institution, documentation may be simply a written statement of explanation by the student or an official statement by a doctor or Vocational Rehabilitation counselor. To be certain of the appropriate documentation, the student should check with the institution's financial aid office. By virtue of provisions within the Americans with Disabilities Act (1990) and the Rehabilitation Act (1973), all public and private postsecondary institutions are required to provide reasonable accommodations for students with documented disabilities who request them.

Some special equipment and support services may be available at the postsecondary institution, through public or private community organizations, through the state Vocational Rehabilitation agency, or through organizations for people with disabilities. The student should check with the Student Services Personnel, 504 Coordinator, or Office of Disability Support Services at the postsecondary institution.

Probably the most valuable resource to a new student is the network of students with disabilities already on campus. Students with disabilities who have had similar experiences and similar needs are likely to have practical advice and low-cost solutions to problems that incoming students with disabilities frequently encounter.

Regardless of whether the student is able to obtain any special equipment or services through the institution or elsewhere, it is still important to let the financial aid administrator know of any anticipated expenses. Such information is considered in the determination of the student's financial need, on which all aid decisions are based. It is also important to understand that disability-related expenses that are covered by other assisting agencies cannot also be covered by financial aid from the school.

### How Does Vocational Rehabilitation Fit Into The Financial Aid Process?

Assistance to students with disabilities is often provided by state Vocational Rehabilitation (VR) agencies. In some states, there are two agencies: a general agency and one for people who are blind or visually impaired. In other states, there is one agency serving all people with disabilities. State Vocational Rehabilitation agency titles vary from state to state, and thus may be hard to locate in the telephone directory. You may contact a state education agency, public library, or Governor's Committee on Employment of People with Disabilities for the telephone number and address of your local VR agency.

The local Vocational Rehabilitation agency has VR counselors who can help a person with a disability determine his or her eligibility for assistance. The VR program is an eligibility program, rather than an entitlement program. To be eligible for services, an individual must have an impairment that results in a substantial impediment to employment and can benefit from and requires VR services for employment. The primary goal of a VR counselor is to assist the client in becoming employed; therefore, the counselor will look closely at a student's educational plans in terms of job potential. While initial counseling and evaluation are open to all, the counselor may determine that a client is not eligible for other services based on state agency policies governing economic need, order of selection, or other criteria.

Among the services that may be provided by VR agencies to a student who is a client :

- Help with tuition expenses
- Room and board.
- Transportation/commuting expenses.
- Books and supplies.
- Reader services for people who are blind or who have learning disabilities; interpreter services for people who are hearing impaired; and/or individually prescribed aids and devices.
- Telecommunications, sensory, and other technological aids and devices.
- Other goods and services that help an individual with a disability become employed.

Services provided to an individual must be authorized in advance in an Individualized Plan for Employment (IPE) developed by the client and approved by a VR counselor.

The above items may differ from state to state and may be subject to a test of a client's ability to pay. They require the use of resources from another agency ("comparable benefits") before a commitment of VR funds is made. There are differences between states' VR programs because each participating state administers its own program through the provisions of a state plan that has been developed under the guidelines of the Act and approved by the U.S. Department of Education. For additional information, request *Vocational Rehabilitation Services: A consumer Guide for Postsecondary Students* from HEATH.

**Is There Coordination Between the Vocational Rehabilitation Agencies and the Financial Aid Offices?**

Most states have developed working agreements between state associations of financial aid administrators and Vocational Rehabilitation administrators. These agreements allow for a coordinated effort in providing funds for students with disabilities in participating states. The agreement, or memorandum of understanding, establishes the process a VR agency and postsecondary educational institution will follow in determining the aid to be granted to a VR client/student. It is important to note that the federal Rehabilitation Act, as amended, requires that students served by a VR agency apply for student financial aid.

Through standardized information exchange form, the VR and financial aid offices are kept abreast of what the other is doing. The process is not a simple one; it takes time and requires a constant effort by both offices and the student. Often a student's aid package is recalculated several times as new information is provided by either office.

The best advice for a student with a disability in the quest for financial assistance is to contact as early as possible both the VR agency where the student is a client and the financial aid office of the institution the student plans to attend to be sure to meet both their deadlines. The institution will determine the student's eligibility for financial assistance and develop an award package. Meanwhile, VR will also determine the student's additional disability-related needs and, if possible, award funds. Whatever is not covered by the VR agency can be recalculated by the institution into the student's expenses, and, if funds allow, the student's aid may be increased. Even with excellent cooperation between the financial aid administrator and the Vocational Rehabilitation counselor, there still may be a need for additional family funds or loans.

**Is Financial Aid Available For Graduate Study?**

The increasing importance of graduate or professional degrees has caused concern over the availability of funds for such study. After a student completes an undergraduate degree program, he or she is no longer eligible for certain federal and state funds. Other programs may serve graduate students, but only after all undergraduates have been served. Because there is the expectation of employability after completion of a technical, community college, or undergraduate degree program, state VR agencies may be reluctant to fund graduate studies. Nevertheless, there are sources of funding available specifically for advanced degrees.

Many students use the traditional routes of institutional scholarships in their field of study, part-time or alternate-semester employment, loans, savings, assistantships, and family contributions as the primary routes to a graduate degree. The college's graduate program or academic department can provide information about funding.

### Are There Other Possible Sources of Financial Assistance?

*Supplemental Security Income*

Supplemental Security Income (SSI) is a federal program that provides financial assistance to people who are aged, blind, or disabled and who have little or no income and resources. The amount of SSI payment is dependent on the income and resources of the client. (If the student is under 18, some of the parents; income and resources will be included.) The student should be aware that earnings from work-study or other employment may affect SSI benefits. If the Social Security Administration approves a Plan for Achieving Self Support, the student would be able to set aside income and resources that are being used toward a specific vocational goal (tuition, savings for equipment or other needs) and continue to receive SSI payments. Plans can be developed by Vocational Rehabilitation counselors, public or private social agencies or groups, anyone assisting the student, or by the student. For more information on SSI and the Plan for Achieving Self Support, contact your local Social Security Administration office.

*Social Security Benefits*

The Social Security Disability Insurance (SSDI) program allows workers and eligible dependents to receive monthly cash benefits because of a period of disability. A student who has been employed may file based on his or her own work record. If the parents of a student with a disability have filed for Social Security or if a parent is deceased, the student may also qualify for dependents' benefits based on the parent's work record. For further information on the student provisions and eligibility requirements of the various Social Security programs, contact your local Social Security Administration office.

*Talent Search, Educational Opportunity Centers, and Special Services for Disadvantaged Students*

Talent Search and Educational Opportunity Centers are federally funded programs located at various sites across the country Some are part of a postsencodary institution, and some have been established as part of a private or public organization. These programs were set up to provide counseling and other servicxes to disadvantaged students and students with disabilities. One of the responsibilities of the program is to help place students and sometimes help them negotiate financial assistance with their postsecondary institutions. Many colleges also have federally funded programs for disadvantaged students, including those with disabilities. These programs provide certain services and academic assistance, and may provide financial assistance as well. Because programs vary by campus, check with the college or university of your choice to see if there is a Special Services Program and what services are offered.

For more information on Talent Search, Educational Opportunity Centers, and Special Services Programs, contact the Division of Student Service, 1250 Maryland Avenue, SW, Portals Building, Suite 600, Washington, DC 20202-5249. Information about these programs is also available at: http://www.ed.gov/offices/OPE/HEP/trio/.

*State Programs*

Most states now offer some form of student assistance. To find out the details of state grants and loans, students should contact their high school counselor or college financial aid administrator. For a listing of the agency that offers assistance for higher education in their state of residence, students can go to http://www.ed.gov.offices.OPE/agencies.html.

*Private Scholarships*

A variety of unique situations, which may have nothing to do with disability may make a student eligible for private scholarships. They may include, for example, parents' place or type of work, military experience, and ethnic background, or student's career goals, religious affiliation, or extracurricular activities. Such scholarships may be researched by purchasing or borrowing books about financial aid from a school or public library. Several of these are mentioned in the References Section.

There are very few scholarships available for people whose unique situation is disability. However, HEATH staff have surveyed organizations and foundations across the country and developed a listing of organizations that provide scholarships for people with particular disabilities. Note that the amount of money from a disability scholarship may be token and ceremonial rather than substantial. Disability organization scholarships are generally $500 to $1,000 per year.

In general, the best resource for all students, including those with disabilities, is the financial aid administrator at the colleges being considered. The financial aid administrator has been trained to understand and explain the complex system of financial aid. In addition, the financial aid administrator will be familiar with local, state, and private sources of funding and able to tie these together with institutional resources to create the most advantageous financial aid package for the student.

Keep in mind, however, that any problems encountered in applying to a college or university, or in completing the financial aid application in a thorough and timely manner, could adversely affect the quality of any financial aid package for which a student may be eligible. Students may apply to, and "shop" among, several colleges for the most advantageous combination of academic excellence and financial aid available. Due to the lead time involved in the college/financial aid process, "smart shoppers: will begin the process of looking for a college or university and preparing to apply for financial aid up to two years in advance of high school graduation.

Other private scholarship sources are listed below.

- The International Kiwanis Club recommends checking with local Kiwanis organizations to see if they offer scholarships. To find the telephone number of your local chapter, call (317) 875-8755.
- For scholarships offered through the Elks Grand Lodge in Winton, North

Carolina, call (919) 358-7661.
- Local chapters of the Rotary Club offer scholarships for overseas study. Call (202) 638-3555 for more information.
- Call the Lions Club International at (630) 571-5466 to find the telephone number for the District Governor in your area, who can inform you about scholarship opportunities.
- Another possible source of funds is the National Association of American Business Clubs at P.O. Box 5127, High Point, NC 27262; (336) 869-2166.

**Scholarship Search Services**

Entrepreneurs in may cities have established scholarship search services that have information about thousands of scholarships nationwide and that provide—for a fee—lists of those most appropriate for individual clients. These services usually can be found in the yellow pages or from a long-distance information operator in various large cities (San Francisco, New York, Houston, and others) under names such as Scholarship Information Service or Scholarship Search. Be forewarned, however, that the value of the information provided by such services can vary considerably. Therefore, as with any other service for which there is a fee, callers should request a written list of exactly what they will get for their investment and what has been the experience of the business in identifying scholarships for students with disabilities. Remember, as discussed previously, there is relatively little grant money made available on the basis of disability. Thus, search services are not likely to list scholarships specifically intended for students with specific disabilities. Rather, they may identify funds available to students by geographic area; area of student interest; college or university; professional, civic, or religious affiliation; or some other criteria.

The student who is willing to invest some time and effort is likely to be just as successful locating funding sources as any fee-charging search service might be. Information about federal student aid programs is readily available at no charge (see :Selected Resources:), while high school guidance counselors and college financial aid offices are good resources for information about state-based and institutional aid. Also, the reference section of a college or community college library is likely to have guidebooks and directories listing grants and scholarships. It is increasingly common for high school guidance departments, libraries, and colleges to offer computerized scholarship searches at little or no cost. Finally, there are numerous resources about financial aid and scholarships on the World Wide Web, including several search services that charge no fee at all (see the following section, "Internet Searches").

**Internet Searches**

Students with Internet access will find a wealth of information about how to complete the FAFSA, as well as additional grants and scholarships for which they may apply. The following World Wide Web addresses are listed to facilitate an electronic search. Note that may web sites offer additional links to other related sites.
1. Easy Access for Students and Institutions (EASI) offers information about the financial aid system: http://www.easi.ed.gov/.

2. Financial Aid for Students, through the U.S. Department of Education's Office of Postsecondary Education, offers information and links relating to federal student assistance programs: http://www.ed.gov/offices/OPE/students.

3. The Financial Aid Information Page is a comprehensive resource that will connect students with mailing lists, news groups, loan information, and scholarships for special interest groups such as females, minorities, veterans, etc.: http://www.finaid.org.

4. FAFSA Express allows students to download, complete, and file the FAFSA electronically: http://www.ed.gov/offices/OPE.express.html. Or call the FAFSA Express Customer Service Line for more information at (800) 801-0576.

5. College Board Home Page includes an instant profile search of available grants and scholarships: http://www.collegeboard.org/.

6. FastWEB (Financial Aid Search Through the WEB) is a searchable database of more than 180,000 private-sector scholarships, fellowships, grants, and loans. Used by colleges across the United States, fastWEB is now available to you at no charge through the World Wide Web, courtesy of the Financial Aid Information Page and Student Services, Inc.: http://www.fastweb.com.

7. CASHE (College Aid Sources for Higher Education), provided free through Sallie Mae's Online Scholarship Service, is a database of more than 180,000 scholarships, fellowships, grants, loans, internships, competitions, and work-study programs sponsored by more than 3,600 organizations: http://www.saliemac.com/.

8. SRN Express is a free web version of the Scholarship Resource Network (SRN) database that focuses on private sector, non-need-based aid. The award listings in the SRN database contain more detailed information than can be found in most scholarship databases and scholarship directories: http://www.rams.com/.

9. CollegeNET MACH25 is a free Web version of the Wintergreen/Orchard House Scholarship Finder database. This database contains listings of more than 500,000 private sector awards from 1,570 sponsors. The database is updated annually: http://www.collegenet.com/mach25/.

10 The National Association of Student Financial Aid Administrators' (NASFAA)home page includes two free downloadable publications for students and their parents, *Cash for College* and *TIPS: Timely Information for Parents and Students*. The site also contains links to other financial aid-related web sites: http://www.nasfaa.org.

11. College Quest is a comprehensive site devoted to the process of searching, choosing, applying, and paying for college that contains a database of more than 850,00 scholarships and grants for postsecondary study: http://www.collegequest.com/.

## Foundation Center

The Foundation Center, with headquarters in Washington, DC and New York and cooperating collections in nearly 100 cities across the country, can provide the names of private foundations that donate money for particular activities or causes. The Foundation Center has a volume of listings called *Foundation Grants for Individuals* arranged in broad categories. It can be used there or purchased for $65 plus $4.50 shipping and handling. Call (800) 424-9836 to find the address of the nearest cooperating collection.

## Selected Resources

**The Big Book of Minority Opportunities** (1997) edited by Willis L. Johnson, lists employment opportunities, financial aid sources, and career information services for members of minority groups.

Although the volume is not specifically for those with disabilities, many students may find it an important resource. This well-organized directory lists more than 4,000 general sources of financial aid. Programs cited include scholarships, fellowships, and loans for college study; job training and retraining activities; summer employment and internship options; occupational information and career-guidance assistance; and employment skills banks and talent bank services. It is available by prepaying $39.95 plus $1.50 for shipping and handling to Garrett Park Press, P.O. Box 190A, Garrett Park, MD 20896, or by calling (301) 946-2553.

**College Financial Aid for Dummies** (2nd Edition), by Joyce Lain Kennedy and Dr. Herm Davis, while not disability specific at all, is one of the most comprehensive and useful small books available on the subject of utilizing the regular financial aid system to full advantage. Basic terms are defined, and needs for money immediately, soon, and in the future are addressed. Kennedy and Davis, who are especially experiences in clarifying all aspects of financial aid, describe ways to simplify the application process, alternative strategies for financing a college education, and numerous borrowing tips. How to locate scholarships, grants, and other gifts is described, as are several save-ahead plans for those who have a few years before the actual college or graduate school dollars are to be spent. Available at bookstores that carry the "Dummies" series of how-to publications, by calling 1-888-438-6643, or online at http://www.idgbooks.com. The cost is $19.99 plus shipping and handling.

**Dollars for College: The quick Guide to Financial Aid for Students with Disabilities** (1998) edited by Elizabeth A. Olson, is a compendium of 525 listings of organizations (including state rehabilitation services, training programs, some colleges and universities, and organizations serving veterans) that offer some type of financial aid for students with disabilities, or offer programs to train people with or without disabilities to prepare to work in the disability service field. In addition, there are several annotated lists of organizations established to assist people with disabilities in areas other than financial aid. There is a description of Federal Financial Aid Programs, a glossary of Financial Aid Terminology, a section of Useful Books, and contact information for a short list of Associations Concerned with People with Disabilities. The Index assists readers in locating programs of relevance to their own needs. *Dollars for College*, one of a series of special focus books on the subject, is available for $7.95 plus $1.50 for shipping and handling from Garrett Park Press, P.O. Box 190B, Garrett Park, MD 20896; (301) 946-2553.

**Don't Miss Out: The Ambitious Student's Guide to Financial Aid** (2000-01) is one of many special focus guides produced regularly by Octameron Associates. This 192-page book is full of useful strategies, helpful hints, and good solid planning information as well as information on the reauthorization of the Higher Education Act and a brief section about students with disabilities. Others in the series cover academic scholarships, college grants, loans, cooperative education opportunities, admissions, campus visits, and transition from high school to college. *Don't Miss Out* is available by prepaying $9 plus $3 for shipping and handling to Octameron Associates, P.O. Box 2748, Alexandria, VA 22301. The publication can also be purchased online at http://www.octameron.com.

**Financial Aid for Graduate and Professional Education** (1997), by Patricia McWade, is a 14-page pamphlet that provides a comprehensive overview of the topic. How and when to apply, determining financial need, types of aid available, aid for special groups and consolidation are some to the topics covered. Contact information about related resources is included. Available by prepaying $2.35 plus $1 for shipping and handling to Peterson's, P.O. Box 2123, Princeton, NJ 08543-21231 (800) 338-3282. This and other Peterson's publications about financial aid can be purchased online at http://www.petersons.com.

**Financial Aid for the Disabled and Their Families** (1998-2000), by Gail Ann Schlachter and R. David Weber, promises to inform readers about the 900 programs that have been established just for individuals with disabilities or members of their families. The book is a useful and comprehensive resource for librarians and counselors, but promises more than it really delivers. The book is well organized for use since it has chapters about financial aid for people with specific disabilities, and there are sections of each chapter for both undergraduate and graduate education. However, entries are double and triple counted, resulting in inflation of the total umber of scholarships and other aids included. The book is available for $40 plus $5 for shipping and handling from Reference Service Press, 5000 Windplay Drive, Suite 4, El Dorado Hills, CA 95762, or by calling (650) 594-0743. The book can also be purchased online at http://www.rspfunding.com.

**Financing Graduate School** (1996), by Patricia McWade, answers the most frequently asked questions about financial aid for graduate school. Topics include aid eligibility, loan jargon, and information on tax laws pertaining to student loan. Available by prepaying $16.95 plus $3 for shipping and handling to Peterson's, P.O. Box 2123, Princeton, NJ 08543-2123; (800) 338-3282. This and other Peterson's publications about financial aid can be purchased online at http://www.petersons.com.

**Funding your Education** (2000-01), created by the U.S. Department of Education, is a booklet that describes the federal student aid programs. The booklet is widely available in school and public libraries or can be ordered free by writing Federal Student Aid Programs, Box 84, Washington, DC 20044-0084 by calling (800) 433-3243, or by visiting their web site: http://www.ed.gov/prog info/SFA.FYE/.

**Grants for Graduate and Postdoctoral Study** (1998), fifth edition, lists and fully describes a diverse collection of more than 1,400 scholarships and grants usable at the graduate level for the study of nearly every discipline. This well-indexed guide provides practical tips as well as specific details about each award. Available in libraries or by prepaying $32.95 plus $3 for shipping and handling to Peterson's, P.O. Box 2123, Princeton, NJ 08543-2123; (800) 338-3282. This and other Peterson's publications about financial aid can be purchased online at http://www.petersons.com.

**Need A Lift? To Educational Opportunities, Careers, Loans, Scholarships, Employment** (annual edition) is a publication of the American Legion covering sources of financial aid and the financial aid process. Special emphasis is given to programs for children of deceased or disabled veterans, but the information is designed to be of service to all students. The 128-page booklet contains sources of scholarships, cooperative education programs, and career information. Available for $3 from American Legion National Emblem Sales, Attn: Need A Lift, Box 1050, Indianapolis, IN 46206.

**The Parents Guide to Paying for College** (1998), by Gerald Krefetz for The College Board, incorporates the new Taxpayer Relief Act regulations to provide parents with practical advice. The 160-page book covers a range of sound financial management strategies for saving, investing, borrowing, and establishing credit for parents of teenagers as well as young children. Discussed in detail are the HOPE Scholarship, Lifetime Learning Tax Credit, and Educational IRAs. There is an extensive glossary to clarify financial terms, appendixes providing an individual tax table, a gift tax table, an income tax rate schedule for trusts, and information on interest rates and yields. Available by prepaying $14.95 plus a $3.95 handling charge to The College Board, College Board Publications, Box 886, New York, NY 10101-0886. The guide may also be purchased online at: http://www.collegeboard.org.

The U.S. Department of Education's toll-free number (800) 433-3243 / (800) 730-8913 (TTY) may be used by seekers of federal student financial aid information. Toll-free calls from all 50 states and Puerto Rico can be made from 9:00 a.m. to 5:30 p.m. EST, Monday through Friday. Callers will receive a recorded message and will be asked to remain on the line if they need additional information or if they have a specific question.

**Scholarship and Financial Aid Resources**
Electronic Industries Foundation (EIF)
Attn: Marcie Vorac
2500 Wilson Boulevard
Suite 210
Arlington, VA 22201
(703) 907-7500
http://www.eia.org/eif
(limited to high school seniors with disabilities who are pursuing undergraduate studies directly related to the electronics industry)

120

Foundation for Exceptional Children; Stanley E. Hackson Award for Gifted/Talented
Students with Disability
1920 Association Drive
Reston, VA 20191
(703) 620-1054
www.cec.sped.org
(limited to entering freshmen who have a disability)

Foundation for Science and Disability, Inc.
Richard Mankin
Grants Committee Chair
503 NW 89th Street
Gainesville, FL 32607-1400
(limited to science students with a disability entering a master's or doctorate program in
engineering, math, computer science or medicine)

La Sertoma International
21710 South Race
Spring Hill, KS 66083
(913) 686-3000
(limited to graduate students who are preparing for careers to assist people who are blind)

National Clearinghouse on Careers and Professions Related to Early Intervention and
Education for Children with Disabilities; The Council for Exceptional Children
1920 Association Drive
Reston, VA 20191-1589
(800) 641-7824
(703) 264-9476
(703) 264-9480 (TTY)
www.special-ed-careers.org
(limited to those who are preparing for careers within the field of special education)

P. Buckley Moss Society
Harbison Award
601 Shenandoah Village Drive
Suite 1C
Waynesboro, VA 22980
(540) 943-5678
(limited to high school seniors with learning disabilities who are continuing their education beyond high school)

The President's Committee on Employment of People with Disabilities
1331 F Street, NW
Suite 300
Washington DC 20004-1107
(202) 376-6200

Recording for the Blind and Dyslexic
20 Rozelle Toad
Princeton, NJ 08540
(609) 452-0606
(limited to students who are blind or visually impaired or who have learning disabilities)

Tony Orlando Yellow Ribbon Scholarship; National Tourism Foundation
546 East Main Street
Lexington, KY 40508
(800) 682-8886
(limited to students with physical and/or sensory disabilities who are planning a career in the travel and tourism industry)

Very Special Arts Young Soloists Program
Attn: Paul Douglas
1300 Connecticut Avenue, NW
Suite 700 Washington, DC 20036
(800) 933-8721
(202) 628-2800
(202) 737-0645 (TTY)
(limited to students aged 25 and under studying selected musical instruments)

---

This resource paper was prepared under Cooperative Agreement No. H326H980002, awarded to the American Council on Education by the U.S. Department of Education. The contents do not necessarily reflect the views of the U.S. Government, nor does mention of products or organizations imply endorsement by the U.S. Government.

Please visit the HEATH website at www.heath-resource-center.org as the information changes year to year.

# Chapter Ten

# Learning from a Learning Disability: What an Educational Researcher has Learned from His Own Educational Experiences

*Bart Pisha, Ed.D., and Roxanne Ruzic, M.Ed.*

*Editor's Note: Two authors prepared this chapter, which focuses on the life experiences of one of them, Bart Pisha. He and Rozanne Ruzic are colleagues at a Massachusetts organization that focuses on using technology to make the educational experiences of all learners, particularly those with disabilities, more successful. In this chapter, when the authors use the pronoun "I," they are describing the firsthand experiences of Bart Pisha. When they use "we," they are describing their shared opinions or experiences as researchers.*

**Bart Pisha, Ed.D., & Roxanne Ruzic, M.Ed.**

## Bart's Story:  An Introduction

When I sat down to prepare this chapter, I invested a lot of thought in replaying memories of my transition from high school to college, applying what I've learned in the 35 years since I graduated from high school in 1965.  I hope that my efforts to capture that experience will seem relevant to today's students.  Further, I hope that the examples I'll mention will help you understand how technology is currently benefiting a group of high school and college students who must struggle to learn well in school.

After an undistinguished career as a student in a well regarded suburban high school, I graduated in June 1965.  I placed in the bottom 20 percent of the class with terrible grades in challenging classes, but my SAT scores were good.  I enrolled in a nearby private liberal arts and engineering college in September 1965, accepted largely because my father had earlier graduated from the same college with honors.  At the end of my freshman year, in June 1966, I was dismissed from this college for "academic deficiencies."  I thought of this as "flunking out."  My parents were not surprised, but they we quite distressed.

Today, at 52 years of age, I am certainly "all grown up," certainly "fully formed."  When I consider my current life, family and work these days, I try to keep an important idea in mind:  There are many ways to measure "success" or "happiness" in life; the definition of these wholly depends upon what really matters most to the individual doing the defining and the measuring.  That's why our country's Declaration of Independence emphasizes "life, liberty, and the pursuit of happiness" but leaves the definition of these important concepts open to discussion.

Today, I hold a doctorate in Education from Harvard University, and I'm employed as Director of Research for CAST, a not for profit educational research and development organization in Peabody, Mass.  I've held my interesting and exciting job at CAST for 15 years, but it still seems terribly hard at times.  I drive a reliable car and live in a comfortable house with my wife and three almost-grownup children.  I go somewhere interesting for a vacation every summer and am able to save a little bit of money  monthly for my retirement years.  I'm not bragging:  The point is that I had a difficult time in schools, persisted and learned to be strategic, found ways to use technology in creative and useful ways, and eventually got a great education.  I have a fulfilling life, and I've learned a lot about ways that I and others who have a learning disability can "work smarter" and succeed in college.  I hope that some of the ideas in this chapter will prove useful to others.

## Transitioning from high school to college: a world of differences

Because no two human beings are alike, no two students' experiences transitioning from high school to college are the same.  This is true for even identical twins, whose biology is markedly similar, but whose personalities and approaches to life are often quite different.  Young adults arrive for the first day of college looking different from each other, wearing different clothes, with different interests, experiences and backgrounds.  One size of life does not fit all; most people like ice cream, but plenty of other people don't.

Most colleges take some steps to accommodate the differences among their students. In addition to the large, required courses all student must take, most colleges recognize the differing learning interests and needs of their students by offering options in the material available for study and perhaps in the methods available to support learning. However, a handful of time-honored learning activities comprise the bulk of the college curriculum.

College students are expected to attend classes, listen to professors' lectures, and take notes. Sometimes students participate in hands-on laboratory sessions, particularly in the physical sciences. The best guide to any particular college course is the professor's syllabus, which contains course assignments and exam dates, and lists textbooks that each student is expected to read and understand. To demonstrate their understanding, students must identify topics suitable for research papers, locate and organize information to build arguments, and solidify these arguments into written papers. Most courses also require students to pass written exams, testing their knowledge of course material. Taken together, college courses have a formidable and relatively rigid body of requirements, challenging for any young person, but frequently overwhelming for the student with learning disabilities.

Based on our experiences in educational research, we believe the college experience can be structured to better meet the needs of students with learning disabilities and other individual differences. Through the use of a concept called Universal Design for Learning™[1] (UDL), developed at the organization where we work, some of the rigidity of courses can be eased without compromising the rigor and value of the college experience.

Learning materials and environments that are created using the UDL approach are designed from the beginning with a much more inclusive view of human potential and needs than is customary. We believe that Universal Design for Learning will do a great deal to individualize the learning experience at all levels of education and will lead to higher rates of success for all students, particularly for students with learning disabilities, by supporting three important learning activities:
1. Recognizing patterns that exist in the flow of incoming information
2. Selecting and applying strategies for working with the information
3. Establishing and maintaining what we call "engagement," the motivation to fully embrace and master the learning task

In a UDL environment, both relatively permanent supports and temporary "scaffolds" for learners who require or desire them are available within the course materials themselves, but they are unobtrusive so that they do not interfere with the work of those who do not need them. Materials allow for choices in presentation of course concepts and students' expressions of their understanding, which means that different students can learn critical material in different ways—ways that make most sense to them— without compromising the rigor of a course. Technology plays a major role in the design of a UDL curriculum; it is difficult to imagine how the needed flexibility could be achieved without it.

Unfortunately, moving from the current rigid and "flat" system towards one that takes into account both the new demands of an Information Age society and the educational potential of new technologies for different learners is slow. A curriculum that incorporates all the elements of Universal Design for Learning does not yet exist. However, beginning in 1993, with the release of Wiggleworks[2], materials for early readers (NOT for college students) with at least some elements of UDL environments have begun to appear and increasingly gain acceptance as mainstream tools for teaching and learning. We have every reason to believe that this trend will continue.

Still, as promising as these developments are for learners over the long term, critical, unfulfilled needs remain, including in the college environment. Today's students with diverse learning needs cannot wait for the development of fully universally designed curricula and materials. Instead, we suggest that students adopt those aspects of universal design that currently exist when and where possible, and apply existing tools and techniques such as "assistive" or "adaptive" technology to improve their abilities to access and learn from curriculum materials in their current forms. While this approach is certainly suboptimal and unlikely ever to lead to the levels of accessibility that UDL promises, much can still be done with tools already at hand.

Supportive technologies, like most tools, will not in and of themselves solve important problems facing users. Rather, it is the student's basic intelligences and task persistence, combined with tools and strategies, that can make success possible. Aside from giving students a sense of personal power and a reason to believe that they can succeed, for instance, we don't think that there's much that technology can do to improve task persistence. Each student must provide the persistence. However, assuming that the student will invest at least a moderate degree of commitment and task persistence in the college experience, we will show how currently available tools and techniques can provide powerful supports for students with learning disabilities who are willing to persevere.

**Tools and techniques**

Consider five key activities that a college student must perform in order to be successful.

1. Listen
2. Read
3. Write
4. Organize
5. Remember

These don't always appear as separate tasks; sometimes two or more must be done at the same time. Further, learners will find that some tools are useful aids to help with more than one of these tasks. As you consider the examples in the rest of this chapter, try to keep this in mind, and always be on the lookout for, new ways to use the tools you know.

These five key activities have changed little since the birth of the university during Europe's Middle Ages, and there is little reason to believe that these cornerstones of university learning will be supplanted in the foreseeable future. However, the ways in which people carry them out will certainly change with the advent of both pertinent technologies and the continued development of learning environments and tools informed by principles of Universal Design for Learning.

While these five activities may appear trivial or simply "common sense" to some, they frequently present imposing challenges to students with learning disabilities. Difficulty with one or more of these activities has ended the college career of many aspiring scholars.

Both to illustrate the importance of these activities and to provide a framework for discussion of the ways in which current technologies may be applied to support students with learning disabilities, we will employ two, intertwined case studies. The first, the story of Bart, introduced at the opening of this chapter, is based on the perceived and remembered experiences of the first author, who entered a well-respected private college in 1965 and was summarily dismissed from it in 1966 for "academic deficiencies." The second case study, the story of Tony, represents an amalgam of the experiences of several college students of the current era with learning disabilities. The students forming the basis of Tony's story successfully applied various technologies and techniques to help them compensate for their learning differences and succeed in challenging, traditionally structured courses of college level study. The technologies and strategies used by Tony are not to be seen as a list of ingredients that each and every student with learning disabilities MUST have in order to succeed, but rather as a series of available supports whose use should be determined by the individual learner's pattern of strengths and weaknesses and other pertinent factors.

**Bart on note-taking**

Like most of my classmates in this all-male school, I sported a close crew cut hairstyle, went to class regularly, listened to the lectures presented there, took notes, and tried to learn whatever the instructors wanted me to. My high school experience, undistinguished as it was, taught me to purchase a separate spiral bound notebook for each class, and to write down everything in it. However, in college I quickly discovered that strategies that had worked to some extent in high school were hopelessly inadequate in college, because classroom demands had increased.

In high school I'd worked hard to write down by hand everything that the teacher said, and sometimes going over the notes after class to correct errors and highlight key points. With the faster pace of college lectures, though, I simply could not write fast enough by hand to capture everything. I found that taking notes in my three daily lectures led to discomfort from my cramped and over-tight pencil grip. Further, my already marginal handwriting became virtually illegible even to me toward the end of each class. My notes deteriorated as time passed, and by mid-term I had abandoned taking notes at all, opting to rely instead upon memory, listening as carefully as I could to each lecture. My exam scores were terrible, as were my eventual course grades. In retrospect, one can see that I was unable to listen and take notes adequately in class for several reasons, the most important of which was that I wasn't clear about exactly what to write down in my notes and what to omit. Writing *everything* down proved impossible. So I chose to write down nothing. My inability to listen adequately and store what I heard in a useful form contributed to my subsequent academic failure in college.

**Tony on note-taking**

Tony, who entered college in 1999, also found taking notes by hand difficult, but he had learned to use technologies and techniques that allowed him to learn in the lecture hall environment. First, Tony carried a small portable cassette tape recorder (and extra batteries!) to class with him. Prior to the beginning of each lecture he jotted the course name and date on a cassette, inserted it into the machine, and reset the recorder's tape counter to zero. As the lecture began, he started the recorder and turned to take written notes.

Rather than relying upon handwriting, Tony took his notes on an AlphaSmart, a highly durable and relatively inexpensive ($240) portable word-processing computer designed for student use. Because he had learned to keyboard in high school, Tony was able to write much more quickly with this tool than he could possibly hand write, and the results were much more legible. He had been taught to take down as much as he could, but then to go back after class and highlight the most important points. Of course, instructors who provided outlines made Tony's note-taking task much easier. Tony understood that trying to memorize what was said in class was an ineffective technique. He tried to concentrate on capturing the main points.

At intervals, and particularly when he felt that he'd not understood or captured the instructor's points, Tony keyed the tape recorder's counter reading into his notes. Whenever the instructor drew an important diagram, Tony copied it down in his spiral notebook and again noted the tape recorder's counter number.

Upon his return to his dormitory room, Tony connected his AlphaSmart to his desktop computer, opened his computer's word processor, and, with a single keystroke, transferred his notes from the portable to the desktop. He then saved his notes to a file created to store notes from this particular course and named to reflect the class session date[3]. Once the notes were in his desktop computer, Tony deleted the notes for this class in his AlphaSmart to make space for future notes and turned to the saved version.

After scanning his work, Tony decided to use the computer's spelling checker to correct spelling errors. He then went on to insert missing words and otherwise clarify what he'd written. While he could read what he had written, he knew from experience that later, when his memory of the lecture had faded, he might not be able to decipher his work. Using his word processor's highlighting[4] feature, he marked anything that appeared twice or more in his notes in yellow. As he did this, he tested his understanding of each point, or section of the notes. Whenever he found himself puzzled and realized that he did not understand, he turned to the tape recorder. Using the counter numbers that he'd earlier inserted in his notes, he was able to locate the confusing section of the lecture quickly; listening to the entire lecture again was too time-consuming. He replayed the relevant section of the tape several times, and found that, with repeated listening at his own pace, he was able to understand. He updated his class notes on the computer to reflect his new understanding and moved on.

Eventually, Tony came to a section that, even with this technique, he could not understand. He highlighted this area of the notes in a special way (for instance, using a color reserved for this purpose), so he would remember to bring it up when he met with his study group over the weekend or saw his professor during office hours. At the study group, Tony found that someone else had understood the point that had challenged him; and Tony was able to clarify a few other points that his fellow students had found confusing.

## Bart on reading textbooks

In my first semester, I found myself confronted with reading demands in each of my five courses that far exceeded anything I had ever experienced. I'd never even written in a textbook before, because the practice had been frowned upon by my high school, the books' owner. I had read my high school texts, most of the time—but very slowly. When I came to an unknown word, I just skipped it, hoping context would carry me through. However, the more challenging college material did not provide me with sufficient context with which to decode and comprehend unknown words, and so my comprehension suffered overall. It was not clear to me what to underline, and in some instances I actually drew lines under all but perhaps a couple dozen words on a single page. Before long, I was several reading assignments behind in each course. Too often, I decided to hang out with friends and return to the reading later. The next afternoon, I'd make the same decision, and the next, and the next. In this way, I stopped reading my textbooks, rationalizing that I'd get the needed information from lecture or in an end-of-the-term cram session. Slowly and by degrees, I gave up on the textbook—which, in many instances, is the core material of the course.

## Tony on reading textbooks

Tony, too, faced massive reading demands in his freshman year, but he had been taught how to use technology to ease them. With the help of the Campus Office of Study Counsel, he had gathered the syllabus of each of his courses early, and had arranged to obtain his course books on audiotape. He listened to these tapes as he read along in the texts, making marginal notes where necessary. For English Literature, his most challenging course, Tony had also been able to locate most of the readings on the Internet, in flexible electronic text format. After locating the text on-line and downloading it to his computer, Tony started up the CAST eReader' software. This program "read" the text Tony had downloaded from the Web aloud to him in an artificial but understandable synthetic voice. As the text was read to him, Tony followed the on-screen highlighting, and took advantage of the simultaneous visual and auditory presentation. When appropriate, Tony stopped the computer's reading to take a note. While Tony took electronic notes in several ways, in this instance he selected a section of text, dragged a copy of it to the eReader's notepad, and keyed in a brief comment regarding the importance of the segment that he had just read. Later, Tony named the file with the textbook chapter[5] and saved this notepad file into his English course folder on the computer, where his lecture notes already resided. Sticking to the simple discipline of saving all files for each course in a single folder did not come easily to Tony; he had been taught this technique by a high school English teacher. In college, the habit paid off in that he was able to locate all of his notes from both lecture and reading readily whenever he needed.

Not infrequently, Tony confronted a word in his reading that, even with the support of repeated re-readings by the computer, he could not understand. In most cases these proved to be vocabulary new to him, but in others the confusion came from weaknesses in the text-to-speech technology in use. Either way, however, Tony found a recourse in the dictionary[6]. Because Tony's dictionary was integrated into his computer, not printed on paper, he found it quite usable. First, Tony selected the word he did not recognize from the electronic course textbook, then clicking on an on-screen dictionary icon. Using MicrosoftÆ Bookshelf, Tony examined a small window with a definition of the word and a button that could be clicked to hear the word pronounced via a high quality recording of a human voice. If the definition Bookshelf offered contained other words unknown to Tony, he could get definitions of those words simply by double clicking them. When he was satisfied that he understood the word, Tony was able to copy the word and its definition directly from Bookshelf to the notepad of eReader, thus embedding the new word's definition into the context of his reading and note taking. Once in eReader, the definition and high-quality pronunciation also were available for review and discussion during study group sessions and when reviewing for an exam.

When he wished, Tony could print out his notepad and course notes, creating a single, chronological notebook of all of his notes from lectures, readings, and the Web, that he used to study. Because Tony inserted into his notepad a dated reference to lecture handouts and sketches, when it came time for a final review, he combined all of his course materials files into a single file, which he had "read" to him by his computer. This provided him with a much more compact and meaningful version of the course material than Bart's jumble of paper notebooks, print textbooks, and handwritten notes on stray pieces of paper.

However, even Tony faced a serious problem in the form of inaccessible textbooks for his courses and research material in the library. Often there was not time to obtain books on tape or electronic copies from the textbook publisher before the course, and these materials were seldom available on the Internet. In these cases, Tony had to bite the bullet and convert these printed documents into digital text format himself. To do so, Tony insured that he was either prepared to cut up his textbook or that he had a high quality photocopy of the material he had to read. This was important in that it allowed him to efficiently process the material in his college's automatic sheet-feeding scanner[7]. When he had scanned all of the required pages, Tony used an optical character recognition (OCR) program to convert the image of the page that the scanner created into a new file, containing the textbook's pages in electronic form. Tony then loaded these pages into CAST eReader, had them read aloud by the computer, and integrated them into his notes from other sources and lectures. Tony spent a lot of time scanning, because the process was somewhat finicky and required some monitoring. He discovered that he needed to use the OCR program's spelling checker to correct the errors that inevitably appear in machine-scanned text. His routine results were satisfactory, in that eReader read the passages to him understandably, but they were NOT perfect renditions of the textbook he scanned.[8]

**Bart on writing**

I was able to settle on a topic for my English literature term paper, the Development of the Sonnet. I'd been taught to use index cards to capture ideas to use in my papers, so that I'd be able to organize and explore them in a variety of ways and later use them to support my argument. I had been to the library—in fact, I had spent two days there reading books and articles on this topic as well as I could, while writing whatever seemed important on index cards for later use. Sometimes, I remembered to copy down the bibliographic information as well, but often I forgot. I had almost 150 cards, each with the name and page of the source from which it came, with text copied longhand and verbatim from the book or article. These index note cards, held together with a large rubber band, varied both in legibility and relevance to my topic.

When I decided that I had enough facts for the paper, I left the library and carried the precious stack of index cards back to my dorm room. I spread them out, grouped and regrouped them, and added new cards, annotated in a contrasting color, to suggest relationships and strands of the argument I planned to make. I found this task difficult to do in my dorm room, as the room was small and people walked through frequently. My strategy had always worked in high school, when I'd done it with my Resource Room Teacher, but now, I found myself alone, in a small physical space, facing more complex topics and greater expectations for performance. Now, in an environment with much less support available from teachers and parents, the index card system proved too bulky and cumbersome for the task. However, in the absence of another more effective strategy, I was forced to rely upon what I knew. I settled on an arrangement of the cards into an order the seemed to suggest a thread to me, but its structure was still mostly unclear as I sat down to write my first draft.

In 1965, the most important learning technology I possessed was my Royal electric portable typewriter. Because I'd had the unusually good foresight to take a full year typing course in high school, I could keyboard at 40 words per minute consistently, ignoring errors. This was much faster then I could handwrite, even for brief intervals, and the results of my handwriting efforts were less legible than my typing. My keyboarding ability proved to be an important strength.

I wrote at the typewriter, double-spacing my work on standard white paper. I flipped through my stack of cards, writing steadily in a stream of consciousness until I had generated the required 12 pages for the assignment. Then, with over one-third of my cards remaining, I wrote a conclusion. The paper went in to the professor the next morning, without a bibliography (there was no time, and the style manual was difficult to understand), and came back a week later with many helpful comments and highlighted errors from my professor.

My ideas received a B-, but overall the paper earned only a C-. This was a passing performance on a difficult task, but not a high enough grade to offset some low quiz grades and to raise my grades in the course as I had hoped. If I'd started earlier and had time to do a second draft, I would probably have earned a better grade, but few students my age could be expected to budget their time so logically. Then, too, it would have taken me two hours to even retype my paper, not to mention the time it would take to thoughtfully edit it. I found my grade disappointing, considering the time and effort I spent on the assignment. On my next paper, I found it impossible to marshal even this degree of task focus, and subsequent efforts reflected my decreased commitment and earned unsatisfactory grades.

**Tony on writing**

Tony approached the process of writing a paper on the same theme as Bart's in much the same manner as Bart did, as the result of much the same training and basic aptitude. Because he had access to technological tools and supports, however, Tony was able to work with his ideas and outside reference materials in different ways. From the outset, he was in a position to access and draw upon his notes from lectures and required readings. Here, he was able to find a good deal of basic information, the names of prominent poets of the age, and the titles of particularly important works. Because his notes from class and readings were all collected together in a single course folder on his desktop computer and had been integrated during study group sessions, he readily found these "starting points" for the required search of pertinent literature. Equipped with the correct spellings of a dozen important authors' names and literary terms, he turned to his computer to begin an electronic search for more information.

Tony had come to rely heavily upon electronic sources of information for writing in high school, where his Resource Room Teacher had taught him to use both online library catalogues and Internet search engines. In their current state, these tools still pose formidable challenges to students with learning disabilities, since one must be able to spell search terms correctly as well as scan and evaluate the relevance of the large amounts of text typically returned by most novice searchers. However, Tony was able to evoke CAST eReader's capacity to "read" most text found on the Internet aloud to him. This greatly facilitated his searches, and helped him decide upon whole Web sites and pieces of text from other sites to be either linked to or copied verbatim into a document that he was developing in his eReader notepad. It was difficult for him to make decisions about what to copy, what to reference, and what to discard, and there is little that technology could do to help him with these matters.[9]

Tony organized his notes much as Bart had earlier, except that instead of using index cards, Tony copied and pasted his ideas into idea-map bubbles, rearranging them simply by dragging and drawing connecting lines in the Inspiration™ software program. Here, too, the sheer number of notes, each in its own bubble, was imposing. However, there was no need to lay cards out on a surface, and if Tony wanted to find a particular bubble where a concept was mentioned he simply entered a key word and, using Inspiration's find feature, let the computer locate and display the correct note. Using the program's built-in zoom feature, Tony was able to view all of the notes simultaneously and move notes as necessary to reflect the relationships he discovered. In this way, Tony created and manipulated relatively large idea maps for complex writing tasks such as this research paper. Because he was able to copy, paste, collect, and manipulate many types of information simultaneously in the digital text environment, it was easier, though certainly not simple, for him to keep track of important details such as the Web address where information was located so that he could cite it later in a bibliography[10,11].

Using a relatively modern computer and appropriate software, Tony began to generate his first draft. He had his notes, arranged in an idea map, or outline format, which he used to guide his drafting. This was a critical phase for Tony, because he had to do the hard work of relating the writings and opinions of a variety of different authors and sources to his topic and argument. He had to remember how to construct good expository paragraphs, with clear topic sentences and illustrative examples or points, cited and drawn from his notes, remembering not to copy others' ideas and to cite references appropriately. Because he had learned to keyboard well, both from his high school class and from diligent practicing as he worked on other pieces of writing, this tool worked relatively well for Tony. Keyboarding proficiency helped him at the most mechanical level, relieving him of the need to hand write and recopy draft upon draft. This convenience was extended by the computer's capacity to save what he'd written so that he could revisit it later and make revisions, moves, substitutions, additions and deletions without laborious recopying. His expertise at this mechanical task, combined with his word processor's built-in spelling checker and its ability to "read" his text back to him through the CAST eReader, supported Tony's efforts to make the multiple drafts that he knew would be necessary if he was to turn in a top-notch paper.

Using this strategy, Tony was able to create strong ideas. He earned a B+ for the paper, with comments about some of his paragraphs and sentences, but no deduction for mechanical errors. Among the suggestions made by the graduate student who actually read and graded his paper was that Tony investigate EndNote™ or another program designed to simplify the organization and processing of bibliographic information.[12]

In the end, Tony and his tutors from the Campus Disabilities Services Office went through his paper one last time. By taking this step, Tony demonstrated his understanding that the computer was not a match for another, relatively uninvolved, peer editor's ability to show him where his writing was strong and where it was weak in communicating and supporting his ideas.

Tony experimented with a speech recognition program to see if it would help him with his writing. In theory, by using this kind of program, individuals can dictate what they want to write into a special microphone attached to their computer. Then, the computer will recognize the words that the writer is speaking and actually write these words into a word processing program for the student. In this way, a lot of typing and correction of misspellings can be saved.

Tony abandoned his speech recognition program after a week or two of use, because he found that he did not have the patience that the program requires for good results. First, Tony needed to "train" the program so that it would recognize his individual voice. This required about 45 minutes of reading passages from the instruction manual in as normal a tone of voice as possible. Tony found the reading difficult, because his reading skills were weak and the text selections were quite challenging. Because he made many mistakes, he had to read several parts of the passages over and over, until he read them correctly. Once he'd completed the training period and began to use the program for writing, Tony found that the program did a pretty good job of capturing his words, but it still made mistakes. Although the manual clearly said that it is important to correct all of these recognition mistakes immediately, Tony usually ignored them, kept right on dictating, and corrected all of the program's errors later, using his word processor.

This seemed to work for a while, but then Tony noticed that the speech recognition program seemed to be making more and more mistakes. Tony did not know that the program keeps learning about the user's voice each time that it is used. This is meant to help the program get better and better at accurately recognizing what the user is saying. However, because Tony did not correct the program's recognition errors right away, the program did not recognize its errors as mistakes. So, instead of using Tony's words to improve its accuracy, the program tried to use words that were actually incorrect to improve its performance and actually began to do a worse job. Tony quickly lost patience with this performance, and stopped using the program.

**Bart on organizing**

I didn't feel that I was particularly disorganized when I began college, even though I clearly was. Others, observing me during high school, saw many clear examples of my disorganization. Both my teachers and my parents attributed my chaotic performances as "laziness." Regrettably, I took these reports as the truth. I came to believe that I was lazy, and that this critical character flaw was at the root of all of the difficulties I experienced in school. So, believing that I was constitutionally lazy, I lost what remained of my motivation to engage with studies, and my performance deteriorated still further.

I often failed to complete homework assignments, and if I did complete one I frequently could not locate it when it was time to turn it in. In fact, it was unusual for me to be able to locate most of the materials that I needed—when I actually needed them. Perhaps this was because my locker was always startlingly disorganized; I just stuffed books, papers, food and clothes into it at each change of classes. The next time I opened the locker, a cascade of "stuff" often met me, falling out and on to the floor of the busy, crowded hall. I'd pick my belongings up, jam them back into the locker, and force the door shut. Most of the things that I'd lost were actually in that locker, but they were both impossible to find and very much the worse for wear after multiple cycles of being stuffed in, falling out, getting stepped on and being forced back into the locker.

When I had to write a story or a paper, I never knew just where to start, and I wasted a lot of time trying to decide. When I finally did manage to get something written, it was invariably disorganized, a string of paragraphs that seemed to be related to each other, somehow, but the paragraphs were out of order and in most cases there were no transitions between paragraphs when the subject changed. Because my handwriting was labored and slow, and because I frequently could not find any first draft that I'd written, I almost never wrote more than a single draft for any assignment. I seemed to have a way with words, if one could see past my "creative" spellings and immature handwriting, but given the layers of problems in them, my papers seldom earned grades above a D.

I had an unsophisticated strategy for studying for tests: I simply reread everything I could get my hands on. This included pertinent sections of the course textbook, any handouts that I could find, and whatever I'd been able to get down in my class notes. In the end, I simply hoped for the best.

I was able to reread everything I had to study for each test because I lost most of what mattered. I lost hats and gloves by the dozen. I usually could not locate materials that teachers passed out in class. I lost textbooks, quizzes and homework assignments returned by the teacher, and I even lost my class schedule. Without my schedule, I was frequently late or missed classes entirely at the beginning of each semester. Once I was able to learn my schedule for the semester, I usually made it to class on time, but I was still unable to remember to show up for appointments and other one-time events. These performances lent weight to adults' original conclusion that I was just one exceptionally lazy boy, who could do great things if I but wanted to. Teachers became frustrated with their inability to change my problem behaviors, and some, most particularly my sadistic gym teacher, gave vent to their frustrations through sarcastic remarks, after-school detention, and other heavy-handed punishments.

Perhaps because I was frequently criticized publicly by my teachers, either for not being able to produce whatever I was supposed to have at the moment or for my "laziness," many of the other students came to pick on me. They often called me unflattering names and cracked cruel jokes at my expense. Sometimes students tripped me or knocked my untidy collection of books and papers out of my hands at a critical moment. This pattern of daily public humiliation at the hands of my teachers and fellow students led to the steady buildup of a fierce and burning anger that periodically burst forth, resulting in shouting matches and fistfights that I usually lost. By the middle of high school, my closest friends were high school dropouts and other students who, like me, were marginalized and miserable—the school's outcasts and losers.

When I moved on to college, I left behind the peers who tormented me and the teachers whom I could not satisfy. I saw this as an important opportunity to shed my old identity, discipline myself to "stop being so lazy" and begin anew. Initially both my hopes and my resolve were high. I struggled mightily to reform myself and scraped through the first semester of my freshman year with marginal, though passing, grades, but I was unable to sustain this level of energy during the second semester. I lacked organizational strategies that might have enabled me to "work smarter, not harder," and so eventually fell back into my familiar old high school patterns. Predictably, my performance was unsatisfactory and I was dismissed from the college, suffering yet another humiliating failure.

**Tony on organizing**

Tony enjoyed two important advantages unavailable in 1965, when Bart started college. First, Tony was identified as having a learning disability early in his school career, and he was taught an array of strategic approaches to common learning and organizational tasks by specialists assigned to help him. Further, Tony owned a personal computer and several other relatively high-tech devices that he'd learned to use to help himself become more organized and productive.

The tool that Tony used to organize his writing, the Inspiration "idea processor," can also be used to organize other information, such as lists of things he needed to do or important points to remember when studying for an exam. As he reviewed his notes, Tony followed traditional methods of identifying what was particularly useful in this material: He reviewed old tests, the syllabus and outlines for each course, discussions in study group, and assignment comments. He then began to create a series of graphic organizers to capture the key elements of each course in a visual metaphor. For literature, he created a diagram in Inspiration, showing the development of the sonnet form over time, with individual nodes representing specific works connected to each poet's name and brief biographical sketch.

The visual nature of these diagrams allowed an additional representation of the relationships among the poets, poems, and developments in the form to be created for the learner. This form incorporated summaries of key points in text, but also added visual representations of information that could be made quite striking and comprehensive, with the addition of various colors, shapes and even images to represent various relationships. Tony sometimes shard these idea maps with a study group, and several members of the study group came to share the burden of creating them.

Much of the benefit that is associated with this sort of study strategy seems to emanate from the grappling phase itself. Any idea map that Tony made proved much more helpful than any he'd gotten from a classmate, unless the map had been discussed in study group. The map's primary value seemed to be as a spark and framing mechanism for discussion in study group. There it was often modified, perhaps on paper copy, and subsequently updated and perfected on the computer, reprinted, and used to guide further study. While Tony favored Inspiration for organizing and for planning writing tasks, some of his friends took a slightly different approach, using an outliner such as More™ or the built-in outlining capabilities of the popular Microsoft Word word processing program. The choice of which electronic tool to use was left up to the individual student, and making that decision usually required a trial period during which both types of programs were used in authentic organizing or writing tasks. For most students the trials were worth the effort, because when they finally settled on a program, they found it a great help in sensibly organizing complicated information.

**Bart on remembering**

I had always had difficulty remembering, and this weakness plagued me in several different ways: I could not readily remember my schedule, and so was often late to class or missed classes altogether. I found it impossible to keep track of all of the little pieces of paper in my life: Appointments, hastily written telephone numbers, business cards, addresses, credit card and bank account numbers, and even the sizes of clothes I wore. During high school I could usually rely upon my parents to help me remember the most important things—doctor's appointments and the dates of SAT exams, for example. I lost a lot of little slips of paper with information or reminders to do things on them, and forgot a great deal of useful or important information. Writing all of this information down in a notebook did not seem to help: Even once it was written in my notebook, I frequently could not find it, and the notebook got very difficult to read both from normal wear and tear and from my crossing out tasks that I'd completed or other information that I no longer needed. However, while I still had access to my parents' help, I was able to manage.

With my entry into college and my move into a dorm room, two important things changed at the same time: I no longer had my parents nearby to remind me of important items, and the number of little bits of information that I needed to keep handy increased dramatically. This type of challenge was and is common among students going to college for the first time, even for those without any identified disability. Many students seem to find ways to cope by themselves, but others are overwhelmed by the complexity of the task. I, like many students with learning disabilities, found myself unable to manage and remember important information in a college environment, and so I missed classes and appointments, lost phone numbers, and was inconvenienced in many other ways. This problem alone probably would not have made college life impossible for me, but, because of all of the other weaknesses I brought to college, this deficit seemed like the last straw. I felt helpless and overwhelmed. I never seemed to know what I needed to do next. Everything I required to get by in college seemed impossibly difficult. When the dreaded letter informing me that I'd been dismissed from the college for "academic deficiencies" finally came, I actually felt relieved that the struggle to stay in college was over.

**Tony on remembering**

Tony also has a great deal of difficulty remembering the same sorts of things that Bart struggled with. Tony relied heavily on his Palm organizer, a pocket-sized, battery-operated computer that Tony could operate with a pen-like stylus. He could enter information into this computer either by writing with the stylus on the Pilot's plastic screen, or by typing the information into Palm software on his desktop computer. Because the desktop computer had software that allowed it to connect through a cable to the Palm and "synchronize," Tony could enter information either way and be confident that it would be available on both computers. When Tony was in his dorm room, he used the Palm program on his desktop computer to categorize and file small bits information from many sources—phone numbers, doctor's appointments, his entire course schedule, dates that important assignments were due. After he synchronized the two computers, Tony could carry all of his information with him, on his Palm. If he picked up some new information while away from his dorm room, he could enter it into the Palm with its stylus. Tony was careful not to lose his Palm, since it was expensive. However, if he knew that if he nonetheless did lose the Palm, he would not have lost all of his information as well. His data would still be stored on his desktop computer, and he could at least work with them on that machine until he either bought a new Palm or decided to take a different approach to remembering.

In addition to simply storing a large amount of information for use anywhere, anytime, Tony also used his Palm to remind him when it was time to do specific important things. For instance, when Tony entered a doctor's appointment or the time and date of a final exam into his Pilot, he also specified that he'd like to be reminded by the unit's making a buzzing or ringing sound to get his attention. Tony also used his watch, which has an alarm feature, for this purpose. The Palm did a better job than the alarm watch, because in addition to making a sound at a designated time, the Palm also flashed information about the appointment or task on its screen. Further, the unit could be set to notify Tony well in advance of an important appointment, and to remind him of what he needed to do to prepare for the appointment.

A good example of the approach Tony used to organize what he needed to remember was a strategy that he developed for working steadily on long-term assignments, such as lengthy research papers. When Tony received a major writing or study assignment, he first entered its due date, with an alarm to remind him the day before, into the Palm. Then, using the Palm's built-in calendar, Tony decided upon and made entries for important milestones and checkpoints when key parts of the task needed to be done. For a research paper, Tony might enter several checkpoints with individual alarms, perhaps a week apart. These might include a date by which he should have done all of his library work, reading and note-taking, a date when he should have his first draft written, a date when his bibliography should be completed, and the date when the final draft of his entire paper had to be submitted.

Tony had considerable success using this tool to help him remember, but it was certainly not perfect. Sometimes Tony tended to put off doing things that his reminders prompted him to complete. In those cases the tool worked, but Tony chose not to use it as he'd planned. Tony got help to remember what to do, but chose not to do it and had to face the consequences. On another occasion, Tony lost his Palm and had to work without it until one of his fellow students found it in the library and returned it to Tony.

What can we learn from the cases of Bart and Tony?

All of these strategies take an inordinate amount of time. It is simply unrealistic to imagine that any young college student would be able, both cognitively and from a financial standpoint, to undertake all of the individual adaptations that Tony adopted. If one could, then assistive technology would be sufficient and we'd have no need for a learning environment that is universally designed.

What students need to do is assess their goals and the requirements of each course, perhaps talking directly with the instructor to determine what the specific learning expectations are for the course. Then, the student can decide:

- What will be most important for me to accomplish in the course? (For instance, knowing the five major causes of the Civil War and to be able to discuss them with a peer may be a better idea than mechanically completing all reading assignments in the syllabus without deciding what's most important and remembering that information. Maybe the former does not require

that the student do all of the reading)
- What are my greatest personal strengths and weaknesses, as they may apply to each course's requirements? (What will I need to develop a strategy toward? What can I safely assume will work well under ordinary circumstances?)

One of the greatest lessons of college that the individual student can learn is how to get by without doing everything that's supposedly expected of each student. This is a part of learning how to learn and think for oneself. Prioritizing and developing strategies to meet the specific content goals of knowledge and understanding is much more valuable and useful than figuring out how to achieve all of the process goals, such as reading everything on a syllabus.

These are lessons from a successful college experience—and they are also lessons for life.

## *Chapter Notes*

[1] Universal Design for Learning is trademarked by CAST to protect the meaning of its approach to improving educational outcomes for all learners, including those with disabilities. However, CAST encourages others to engage in the UDL discussion and dissemination. For more information on the permitted uses of UDL, please visit CAST's Web site at www.cast.org.

[2] WiggleWorks, a registered trademark of Scholastic, Inc., was co-developed by CAST and is the first mainstream curriculum material to incorporate supports for diverse learners, such as simultaneous highlighting of text as it is "read" aloud by a high-quality digitized voice, optional enlarged on screen type for individuals with visual impairments, and "notebooks" that allow learners to capture the correct spellings of novel words for use in later writing.

[3] For instance: EngLit021600 for a file created for English literature on February 16 of 2000. Other naming schemes, as long as they are sensible and memorable, will also work.

[4] Most major word processors have features that can highlight text in background color. Alternatively, placing text in bold face or italics can work, as well.

[5] For instance, EngLitTxtChapt3.

[6] Bart, too, might have gone to a dictionary in this situation, but he'd never found dictionaries particularly helpful, and, in the pre-computer era, it took him a long time to look up each word.

[7] The library or Disability Services Office will have one, or should. This device, costing about $500, functions much like a photocopier, in that it can automatically feed a stack of pages through a scanning cycle where an electronic image of each page is made. However, the scanner saves a copy of this picture to the computer's memory, rather than printing it on paper as a copier does. As UDL becomes more widely adopted, this kind of tactical issue will disappear, particularly the scanning and OCR rendition of text.

[8] It requires about 3 minutes to scan and process a typical textbook page. This adds up, and in a "community of scholars supporting each other" model, study group colleagues could split up the scanning and each do a portion for the group.

[9] These intellectual tasks form a major part of what students go to school to learn, and it is largely the process of manipulating ideas repeatedly and looking for interrelationships that leads to the construction of new knowledge for the learner. Technology, however, has a large contribution to make to the process by helping to manipulate ideas and text much more simply and quickly, allowing the student more time and flexibility with which to address his developing ideas.

[10] The techniques of critical thinking must be applied to evaluate information found on the Internet. Even though errors of fact and interpretation occasionally occur in textbooks and other printed references, the Internet makes it possible for anyone to "publish" factually incorrect information and label it as fact.

[11] Unfortunately, new technologies have increased the allure of one of scholarship's oldest curses—plagiarism. Tony had already copied large bits of text from online sources and arranged them in the idea processor. It would have been simple to save the idea map as a text only document, format it, and hand it in as original work. As Tony knew, this was unacceptable, and was far removed from true scholarship and learning. Still, we note that modern computer technology only exacerbated a problem that has existed since the dawn of the print book, and both historical and contemporary examples abound. Technology has, however, made plagiarism vastly simpler and quicker to perform, and so perhaps more tempting to the student. Here, too, the responsibility to invest the required effort and to struggle honestly with difficult ideas in a difficult format resides squarely with the student. We hope that students' resolve to synthesize new knowledge for themselves, rather than simply plagiarize others' ideas, will prove sufficient to help them avoid this pitfall. Perhaps students' resolve will be strengthened by the knowledge that any text they've collected from an online source can be located just as easily by an instructor. It's quite easy to enter a unique portion of the "student's" text into a search engine and examine the results.

[12] Bibliographic information can be stored in EndNote correctly once a relevant passage is discovered, and this reference can be pasted directly into a word processing document, near where Tony has written about the ideas he found in that particular book or article. Once in EndNote, the reference can be inserted in a paper with a simple copy and paste, and a bibliography, formatted in any of a number of recognized bibliographic styles, can be created almost effortlessly. Notes, URLs, scanned articles and pages can also be linked to the reference citation, so that a web of information, accessible through a variety of routes, is created. Though EndNote deals with text, which is inherently difficult for people like Bart and Tony to access, the text can be read aloud by the computer. Most word processing programs also allow aspiring authors to insert "voice notes" directly into documents, using the computer's standard microphone and sound card.

## Some final thoughts on transitioning from high school to college

- Meaningful college-level academic study is hard work. If you have what is often called a "learning disability" and you want to succeed in a rigorous college, you are going to have to work much harder than many of your peers who do not share your individual array of strengths, weaknesses, blessings and curses. Get down, get a grip, get used to it, and get a clear picture of reality. If you're not ready to work in college, we suggest that you go out and get yourself a job. You'll save your parents and yourself a lot of money and grief, and you can always go later if you change your mind.

- Figure out what interests you. Think carefully about what you'd like to know more about, and arrange your courses so that you'll spend most of your time studying things that interest you.

- Learn as much as you can about yourself as a learner. This is harder to accomplish than it sounds. If you discover that you cannot read with noise nearby, find a quiet place to study. If you always forget your notebook for your morning class, put it in your backpack the night before. Find out what you need, and provide it for yourself.

- Almost all successful authors write multiple drafts, improving their works as they rewrite them, and you'll need to do this in college. Get used to this, too.

- There are lots of strategies, or "tricks" that successful students sometimes use to learn better and faster. You don't know all of them, and learning a few more will be worth your time.

- Do your best to learn the difference between a string of words and an idea, and then collect other people's ideas to understand and to write about in your papers. If you use other people's exact words or key ideas in a paper of your own, learn how to give the others proper credit in academic writing!

- Never simply copy other people's words into anything you submit in college, except when you absolutely must. Then, be sure to directly quote and cite the original author. Copying other's work is called plagiarism. Plagiarism can get you expelled from any college, and even if you are not caught, it will not help you to learn.

- If you don't know how to type or keyboard as rapidly as you can write with a pen, start learning now. Learn to use the "correct" finger on each key, and 10 minutes of practice every day with almost any typing tutorial program will help you improve your skills quickly

- Use technology to help you think and put ideas together. Technology has several capabilities that may make it useful for these tasks. For instance, using a computer and an "idea processor" or outliner can make it much easier to organize your thoughts and information before writing a paper.

- Use technology to perform repetitive tasks. For instance, use a word processing program to make it easier to create multiple revisions of the same paper.

- Use technology to build yourself a temporary "scaffold," just as construction workers do, so that you can work on the highest-level aspects of college-level learning. Many experts believe that this is the key to success, Get all of the support you can on the things many students with learning disabilities are terrible atóspelling, reading written words, getting organized, rememberingóso you can liberate your strengths: thinking, seeing relationships, understanding relatively large bodies of information, learning from experience.

- Don't be too afraid to take *some* chances. Some risk is involved in virtually every important experience that anyone ever has.

# Appendices

**Source: U.S. Department of Education**

**Anything can happen! Investigate the possibilities in** *"Think College? Me? Now?"*

For those who do not have immediate access to the internet, the following information is excerpted from:  Think College Early produced by U.S. Department of Education.  For much more information on the topic, call or write to:
U.S. Department of Education
600 Independence Avenue, SW
Washington, DC 20202
1-800-USA-LEARN

For those with computer access at home, or at the school or local library, go to the U.S. Department of Education Web site:
**http://www.ed.gov/pubs/GettingReadyCollegeEarly/**

*"Think College? Me? Now?"*
You?  Think about college now in middle school or junior high?  Yes!  It's time to think about <u>why you should, even if no one in your family ever went to college</u>.  If you learn differently or have special needs you also need to start planning for college early.

By college we mean education after high school.  This includes 2-year community or junior colleges, business schools and vocational technical schools as well as 4-year colleges and universities.

We don't mean you need to know exactly what you want to be when you grow up.  It's OK not to know yet.  But it's time to start thinking about what you like to do, what you're good at, and what makes you happy.  Things like that.  Those things can give you clues to what you might like to explore in education after high school and in the world of work.

**Why should you think about education after high school?**
 Because it can be the key to the kind of future you want.  Education gives you choices that you might not otherwise  have.  More and more good jobs depend on the skills and knowledge that education after high school can provide.  Staying in school and going to college will help you:
* be in a better position to help your family and your community;
* get a better job and earn more money;
* and get a good start in life!

Even if you're not sure what your future holds, prepare AS IF you are going to college.

## Make Sure That All Courses Meet High Standards

It is not only important for your child to enroll in the courses recommended for college-bound students; it is also essential that the material taught in those courses reflect high academic standards and high expectations for what students should know and be able to do. Research indicates that high expectations and high standards improve achievement and positively influence student learning.

Efforts are under way in states and communities across the country to answer the question: *"What is it that our children ought to know and be able to do ... to participate fully in today's and tomorrow's economy?"* Many states and local communities have been developing or revising their standards (sometimes called "curriculum frameworks") in core subject areas such as math, science, English, history, geography, foreign languages, civics, and the arts. These standards help provide parents with answers to questions such as:

*"Is my child learning?"*
*"What is it that my child should know by the end of each grade?"*

Many school districts are not waiting for their states to complete standards. In many local communities, groups of citizens —parents, teachers, administrators, business leaders, clergy, representatives from colleges, curriculum experts, and other community members —are working together to develop or revise standards. In creating their own standards, many States and local communities are drawing on model voluntary standards developed by national professional associations.

In order to make sure that the curriculum in your child's school meets high academic standards, call your child's school to find out if State or local standards are being developed. Ask how you can get involved in the standard-setting process. Join with other parents, teachers, and your child's principal and compare your school's standards against the best schools and the best State standards.

## Questions To Ask Guidance Counselors:

- What basic academic courses do they recommend for students who want to go to college?
- How many years of each academic subject does the high school require for graduation?
- What elective courses do they recommend for college-bound students?
- How does a student go about completing recommended courses before graduating from high school?
- Can students who are considering college get special help or tutoring?
- What activities can students do at home and over the summers to strengthen their preparation for college?
- How much homework is expected of students preparing for college?
- What kinds of high school grades do different colleges require?

## Getting Ready: Taking the Right Courses for College Starts in Middle School

Everyone knows that high school courses and grades count for admission to college, but many people don't realize that a college education also builds on the knowledge and skills acquired in earlier years. Your child should plan a high school course schedule early, in the sixth or seventh grade.

## Challenging courses help kids get into college

Research shows that students who take **algebra** and **geometry** early (by the end of the eighth and ninth grades) are much more likely to go on to college than students who do not. In a national sample, only 26 percent of low-income students who did *not* take geometry went on to college; but 71 percent of low-income students who took geometry went to college. It is common in other developed countries for students to have mastered the basics of math, algebra, and some geometry by the end of the eighth grade. By taking algebra early in middle and junior high school, students can enroll in chemistry, physics, trigonometry, and Advanced Placement courses before finishing high school.

Just as employers want workers who have certain skills, most colleges want students who have taken certain courses. Many of these courses can be taken only after a student has passed other, more basic courses. The most important thing a student can do to prepare for college is to sign up for the right courses and work hard to pass them. As parents, you should get involved in choosing your children's schedule for the next year, and make sure that your children can and do take challenging courses. College-bound **middle and junior high school students should take:**

- **Algebra I** (in **eighth** grade) and Geometry (in **ninth** grade) or other challenging math courses that expect students to master the essentials of these subjects. Algebra and geometry form the foundation for the advanced math and science courses colleges want their students to take, and give students the skills they need to succeed on college entrance exams, in college math classes, and in their future careers.

- **English, Science and History or Geography** *Every* **Year**. Together with math, these courses make up the "core"—the basic academic classes every student should take *every* year, in middle school and in high school. Students can take a variety of English, science and history classes—all of them good preparation for college. See chart 2 for examples of recommended courses.

- **Foreign Language**. Many colleges require their students to study a foreign language for at least two years, and some prefer three or four years of one language. Taking a foreign language shows colleges that a student is serious and willing to learn the basics plus more, and shows employers that he or she is prepared to compete in the global economy.

- **Computer Science**. Basic computer skills are now essential, and more and more jobs require at least a basic knowledge of computers. Make sure your child takes advantage of any opportunities the school offers to learn to use computers.

- **The Arts**. Many colleges view participation in the arts and music as a valuable experience that broadens students' understanding and appreciation of the world

145

around them. It is also well known and widely recognized that the arts contribute significantly to children's intellectual development.

## Typical High School Courses Recommended for Four-Year College

### English: 4 years
*Types of classes:*
composition
American literature
English literature
world literature

### Mathematics: 3 to 4 years
*Types of classes:*
algebra I
geometry
algebra 11
trigonometry
pre-calculus
calculus

### History & Geography: 2 to 3 years
*Types of classes:*
geography
U.S. history
U.S. government
world history
world cultures
civics

### Laboratory Science: 1 to 3 years
*Types of classes:*
biology
earth science
chemistry
physics

### Visual/Performing Arts-1 year
*Types of classes:*
art
dance
drama
music

### Challenging Electives: 1 to 3 years
*Types of classes:*
economics
psychology
computer science
statistics
communications

### Foreign Language: 2 to 3 years

## Get a "Leg Up" on College Preparation
High school students can also take courses for credit at many colleges. These courses—Advanced Placement and Tech-Prep—are available in the tenth, eleventh, and twelfth grades. Middle school and junior high school students who plan ahead and take algebra, a foreign language and computer courses by the eighth grade can be better prepared for Advanced Placement and Tech-Prep courses in high school.

**Taking Advanced Placement (AP) courses**. AP courses are college-level courses in 16 different subjects that help students get ready for college during high school. Students who score high enough on the AP exams can get advanced placement in college or college credit.

**Taking "Test-Prep" courses**. Students who want to pursue a technical program at a community, technical, or junior college may want to prepare by taking some technical courses in high school in addition to the core courses. Talk to someone at your child's school or from a community, junior, or technical college to find out the best high school courses to take for tech prep involvement.

## Take the Standardized Tests That Many Colleges Require

Many of the courses recommended for college-bound students (such as geometry and rigorous English courses) are also essential preparation for the college entrance examinations —the SAT I (Scholastic Assessment Test) or the ACT Assessment. The SAT I measures verbal and mathematical reasoning abilities. The ACT Assessment measures English, mathematics, reading, and science reasoning abilities. Students applying to colleges in the East and West usually take the SAT I exam. Students applying to schools in the South and Midwest often take the ACT. (However, students should check the admission requirements at each school to which they are applying.)

Usually, the tests are offered in the junior and senior years of high school and can be taken more than once if a student wishes to try to improve his or her score. Students can get books at libraries or bookstores to help them to prepare for all of the tests. Some of these books are listed at the end of this section. In addition, some private organizations and companies offer courses that help students prepare for these exams.

Many schools offer the Preliminary Scholastic Assessment Test/National Merit Scholarship Qualifying Test (PSAT/NMSQT) to their students. This practice test helps students prepare for the Scholastic Assessment Test (SAT I). The PSAT is usually administered to tenth or eleventh grade students. A student who does very well on this test and who meets many other academic performance criteria may qualify for the National Merit Scholarship Program. You and your child can find out more about the PSAT/NMSQT and the National Merit Scholarship Program by talking to your child's guidance counselor or by calling or writing to the number or address provided at the end of this section.

Some colleges also require that an applicant take one or more SAT II Subject Tests in major areas of study. It is a good idea for a student to consult a guidance counselor about this early in high school; often the best time to take an SAT II Test is right after the student has taken a course in that subject. For example, many students take the Biology SAT II Test right after they have completed a course in biology. This could mean that your child would take his or her first SAT II Test as a freshman or sophomore in high school.

The SAT. Write or call:
SAT Program
P.O. Box 6200
Princeton, NJ 08541-6200
Phone: 609-771-7600

The ACT. Write or call:
ACT Registration
P.O. Box 414
Iowa City, IA 52243
Phone: 319-337-1270

The Preliminary Scholastic Assessment Test/(PSAT/NMSQT).  Write or call:
PSAT/NMSQT
P.O. Box 6720
Princeton, NJ 08541-6720
Phone: 609-771-7070

## Accommodations for SAT, PSAT, and Advanced Placement (AP)

The College Board provides reasonable accommodations to students with documented disabilities.  When making a request for the testing accommodation, it is necessary to submit a *Student Eligibility Form* as well as the basic Registration Form.  For further information: **http://www.collegeboard.org/disable/counsel/html/indx000.html** There are specific criteria that must be met to be eligible.  This is an area in which parents and students need to seek the assistance of  the high school coordinator in charge and/or special educator, guidance personnel, psychologist who did the diagnostic testing, an educational advocate.

## Books About Preparing for Standardized Tests

Note:     One of the best ways to prepare for standardized tests is to practice with actual tests.  The first two books in the following list focus on copies of previously administered tests.

1.   *Real SATs*.  The College Board, 1995.

2.   *Official Guide to the ACT Assessment*.  Harcourt Brace Press, 1990.

3.   *Barron's How to Prepare for the PSAT/NMSQT*, Eighth Edition, Samuel Brownstein, Mitchel Weiner, and Sharon Weiner Green.  Barron's Educational Series, 1993.

4.   *Barron's How to Prepare for the SATI*, Eighteenth Edition, Samuel Brownstein, Mitchel Weiner, and Sharon Weiner Green.  Barron's Educational Series, 1994.

5.   *Barron's How to Prepare for the ACT*, Tenth Edition, George Ehrenhaft, Robert Lehrman, and Allan Mundsack.  Barron's Educational Series, 1995.

6.   *Preparation for the SAT*, 1997 Edition, Edward Deptula (ed.).  Arco Publishers, 1996.

7.   *Cracking the SAT and PSAT*, 1996, Adam Robinson and John Katzman.  The Princeton Review, 1995.

8.   *Cracking the ACT*, 1996-97, Geoff Martz, Kim Magloire, and Theodore Silver. Princeton Review, 1996.

9.   *Word Smart: Building an Educated Vocabulary*, Adam Robinson.  Princeton Review, 1993.

# Appendix B

**Accommodations**
Testing, Instructional and Programmatic
(Source Riley, 1998)

**Testing Accommodations**

Alternative Setting
- Administer the test in a separate location, individually.
- Administer the test in a location with minimal distractions.
- Administer test in a study carrel, individually.
- Provide special lighting.
- Administer the test to a small group in a separate location.

Time and/or Schedule Changes
- Extend the time allotted to complete the test.
- Allow frequent breaks during testing.
- Consider time of the day best for student.
- Administer the test in several sessions.
- Administer the test over several days.
- Consider a flexible schedule / at different day or week.

Changes in Test Format
- Increase spacing between items and lines or reduce items per page or line.
- Highlight key words or phrases in directions.
- Limit reading passages with one complete sentence per line.
- Allow student to mark responses in booklet rather than on bubble answer sheet.
- Increase size of answer sheet bubbles.
- Employ a reader for directions, with clarification.
- Employ a reader for questions (as appropriate, with or without clarification).
- Request audio tape of test.
- Request test on computer / use of word processor (as appropriate, with or without spell check).
- Have the computer read to the student.
- Give dictation to a proctor/scribe.
- Use a calculator.
- Use a place marker.

Instructional Accommodations
- taped textbooks/ readings
- readers
- note-taking modifications
  * note takers / paid or volunteer list or class member volunteer
  * class member volunteer uses two-copy carbonless paper (plain or graphed
  * for math/science) or notes Xeroxed by student with LD

* tape recorder
* laptop computer
- syllabus and course requirement handouts several weeks in advance
- formative evaluation / feedback prior to final products on assignments
- alternative assignment / equivalent level of challenge
- extended time on assignments
- extra credit assignments
- no penalty for spelling/grammar errors in spontaneous writing, such as for exams, in-class writing or use of portable spell check (except where literacy is requisite)
- tutoring for course content / subject matter / course assignments
- auxiliary aids (personal / library / computer center)

## Program Accommodations

- Interview and review of diagnostic testing with LD service provider (if self-identified)
- Request special housing (e.g., single room or dorm with quiet study areas)
- Seek priority registration
- Seek full time status with minimal reduction in course load (financial aid considerations)
- Seek part-time program / with full-time services, extra-curricular and dorm privileges
- Audit courses (no fee) to be taken in another semester or as prep for a different course
- Consider independent study course for challenge area
- Take review/remedial courses for non-credit or credit (e.g., math, writing)
- Use LD Academic Support Services Center
- Consult the LD Specialist Service Provider/Advocate/Advisor

## Appendix C

**Technological Aids**
Portable Spell-Checker/Dictionary/Thesaurus/Speech: Pronounces Target Word English/ Other Languages

Franklin Learning Resources
122 Burrs Road
Mt. Holly, NJ 08060
800-525-9673

**Talking Calculator**
Sharp Talking Calculator EL-640
Sharp Electronics Corporation
Sharp Plaza
20600 South Alameda Street
Carson, CA 90810
213-637-9488

## Text to Speech

<u>Note:</u> Apple Macintosh computers with System 7 or later are capable of Text to Speech. IBM and compatibles with Windows 95 are capable of Text to Speech, but require an added sound card.

textHELP
HumanWare, Inc.
6245 King Road
Loomis, CA 95650
916-652-7253

Kurzweil 3000
Kurzweil Personal Reader
HumanWare, Inc.
6245 King Road
Loomis, CA 95650
916-652-7253

## Scanner

Epson America, Inc.
20770 Madrona Ave.
Mail Stop C2-02
Torrance, CA 90509-2843
310-782-2600
800-463-7766

Hewlett Packard Company
3000 Hanover St.
Palo Alto, CA 94304-1185
650-857-1501

Microtek Lab, Inc.
3715 Doolittle Dr.
Redondo Beach, CA 90278-1226
310-297-5000
800-654-4160

## Recorded Texts

<u>Computerized Books</u>
Computerized Books for the Blind
37 Corbin Hall
University of Montana
Missoula, MT 59812
406-243-5481

<u>Recorded Books</u>
Library of Congress
National Library Service for the Blind and Physically Handicapped
1291 Taylor St., NW
Washington, DC 20542
202-707-5100

Recorded Books
Recording for the Blind & Dyslexic
20 Roszel Road
Princeton, NJ 08540
609-452-0606
http://www.rfbd.org

## Four-track Tape Recorders / Variable Speech Control

Handi-Cassette
American Printing House for the Blind, Inc.
1839 Frankfort Avenue
P.O. Box 6085
Louisville, KY
502-895-2405

Recording for the Blind & Dyslexic
20 Roszel Road
Princeton, NJ 08540
609-452-0606
800-221-4792
http://www.rfbd.org

GE Fastrac
General Electric
P.O. Box 1976
Indianapolis, IN 46206
800-447-1700

## Speech to Text

Dragon Dictate
Dragon Systems, Inc.
320 Nevada Street
Newton, MA 02160
617-965-5200

VoiceType Simply Speaking
IBM
Old Orchard Road
Armonk, NY 10504

## Graphic Organizing Software: Generate and Organize Ideas through Mapping, Webbing, Outlining

Inspiration
Inspiration Software, Inc.
2920 SW Dolph Court, Suite 3
Portland, OR 97219
503-245-9011

## Proofreading Software

Grammatik IV
Reference Software
330 Townsend Street, Suite 123
San Francisco, CA 94107
415-541-0222

Correct Grammar
Writing Tools Group
1 Harbor Drive, Suite 111
Sausalito, CA 94965
415-332-8692

## Personal Data Manager:  Software

WordPerfect Library
WordPerfect Corporation
1555 N. Technology Way
Orem, UT 84507
801-225-5000

## Personal Data Manager:  "Stand Alone"

Texas Instruments Pocket Solutions Data Banks
Texas Instruments
P.O. Box 2500
Lubbock, TX 79408
806-747-1882

**Mouse Interface Software**
MousePerfect
MousePerfect, Inc.
P.O. Box 367
Clarston, GA 30021

**Key Repeat Inhibitor**
Filch
Kinetic Designs
14321 Anatevka
Olalla, WA 98459
206-857-7943

## Appendix D

Source: Durlak, Christine M. (1992). Preparing high school students with learning disabilities for the transition to post secondary education: Training for self-determination. Dissertation Abstracts International. Vol. 53(6-A), Dec (pp. 1866). (adapted with permission of author)

The following two instruments are included here to inform students about the kinds of behaviors being referred to when professionals speak of terms, such as self-advocacy and self-awareness. Since self-understanding regarding these skills is the real goal, students might find it valuable to rate themselves with these instruments and discuss the topics with a mentor or peer.

### Self-Advocacy Checklist

*Instructions*:  This evaluation asks you to examine your skills in the area of self-advocacy (assertiveness and interpersonal skills).  Please read each statement and indicate how you think you compare to other students your age in these specific areas.

| | |
|---|---|
| 5 = Very High | 2 = Below Average |
| 4 = Above Average | 1 = Very Low |
| 3 = Average | N/O = Not Observed |

1.   Recognizes he or she needs help
2.   Knows when and how to request help
3.   Participates verbally in class (appropriately)
4.   Makes eye contact with person to whom speaking
5.   Is aware of kinds of accommodations available for testing and other needs and understands which are appropriate for his/her characteristics (e.g. oral exams, extended time for tests, books on tape)
6.    Asks appropriate help from peers
7.   Actively participates in setting, establishing, and discussing IEP goals (this question for special education faculty only)
8.   Speaks in appropriate voice tone for situation

9.   Cooperates when asked
10.  Persists when necessary
11.  Asks questions if doesn't understand
12.  Works independently
13.  Indicates confidence in academic abilities
14.  Initiates work, participation, questions
15.  Volunteers answers in class
16.  Indicates confidence in social abilities

## Self-Awareness Checklist

*Instructions*: This evaluation asks you to examine your behavior in certain areas. Please read each statement and indicate how you think you compare to other students of your age in these specific areas.

| | |
|---|---|
| 5 = Very High | 2 = Below Average |
| 4 = Above Average | 1 = Very Low |
| 3 = Average | N/O = Not observed |

1.   Communicates well with teachers
2.   Takes responsibility for personal behavior
3.   Defines the term learning disability and how it affects him/her personally
4.   Demonstrates self-confidence in social situations
5.   Describes strengths and weaknesses to you (academic and social)
6.   Realistically assesses abilities, future goals
7.   Demonstrates a willingness to accomplish goals
8.   Communicates well with peers
9.   Demonstrates an awareness of consequences of his/her behavior

# References

**Chapter 1 Johnson**

Johnson, D., & Blalock, J. (1987). *Adults with learning disabilities.* Orlando, FL: Grune & Stratton.

Lauren J. (1997). *Succeeding with L.D.* Minneapolis, MN: Free Spirit Publishing Co.

Smith, S. (1994). *Different is not bad: Different is the world; A book about disabilities.* Longmont, CA: Sopris West.

Shaughnessy, M. (1977). *Errors and expectations.* New York: Oxford University Press.

**Chapter 2 Riley**

Baker, J M. & Zigmond, N. (1995). The meaning and practice of inclusion for students with learning disabilities: Themes and implications from the five cases. *Journal of Special Education,* 29(2), 163-180.

Borkowski, J.G. & Muthukrishna, N. (1992). Moving metacognition into the Classroom: "Working models" and effective strategy training. In M. Pressley, K. R. Harris & J.T. Guthrie (Eds.), *Promoting academic competency and literacy in school.* (pp. 477-501). Toronto: Academic Press.

Boudah, D., Schumaker, J. & Deshler, D. (1997). Collaborative instruction: is it an effective option for inclusion in secondary classrooms? *Learning Disability Quarterly,* 20, 293-316.

Brown, R. & Pressley, M. (1994). Self-regulated reading and getting meaning from text: The transactional strategies instruction model and its ongoing validation. In D. Schunk & B. Zimmerman, (Eds.), *Self-regulation of learning and performance: Issues and educational applications.* (pp. 155-179). Hillsdale, NJ, USA: Lawrence Erlbaum Associates, Inc.

Bulgren, J., Schumaker, J. & Deshler, D. (1994). The effects of a recall enhancement routine on the test performance of secondary students with and without learning disabilities: *Learning Disabilities Research & Practice,* 9, 2-11.

Bursuck, W., Munk, D. & Olson, M. (1999). The fairness of report card grading adaptations: what do students with and without learning disabilities think?: *Remedial and Special Education,* 20, 84-92.

Bursuck, W., Polloway, E., Plante, L., Epstein, M., Jayanthi, M. & McConeghy, J. (1996). Report card grading and adaptations: A national survey of classroom practices: *Exceptional Children,* 62, 301-318.

Butler, D. (1995). Promoting strategic learning by postsecondary students with learning disabilities: *Journal of Learning Disabilities*, 28, 170-190.

Capital Publications. (1997). Special education dropout rate remains stagnant: *Special Educatin Law Repoter*, 23(1), 1-2.

Cain, K. (1996). Story knowledge and comprehension skill. In C. Cornoldi & J. Oakhill (Eds.), *Reading comprehension difficulties*. (pp.167-192). Hillsdale, NJ: Lawrence Erlbaum Associates.

Durlak, C. M. (1992). Preparing high school students with learning disabilities for the transition to postsecondary education: Training for self-determination (Doctoral Dissertation, Northern Illinois University, 1992). Dissertation Abstracts International, 53, 1866.

Durlak, C.M., Rose, E. & Bursuck, W.D. (1994). Preparing high school students with learning disabilities for the transition to postsecondary education: Teaching the skills of self-determination: *Journal of Learning Disabilities*, 27, 51-59.

Dweck, C. S. & Leggett, E. L. (1988). A social cognitive approach to motivation and personality: *Psychological Review*, 95(2), 256-273.

Eccles, J. S. & Midgley, C. (1990). Changes in academic motivation and self- perception during early adolescence. In R. Montemayor, & G.R. Adams, (Eds.), *From childhood to adolescence: A transitional period? Advances in adolescent development, Vol. 2.* (pp. 134-155). Newbury Park, CA, USA: Sage Publications, Inc.

Edgar, E. & Polloway, E. (1994). Education for adolescents with disabilities: Curriculum and placement issues: *The Journal of Special Education*, 27, 438-452.

Ellett, L. (1993). Instructional practices in mainstreamed secondary classrooms: *Journal of Learning Disabilities*, 26, 57-64.

Elliott, J. (1993). If it is "dynamic" why is it so rarely employed?: *Educational and Child Psychology*, 10(4), 48-58.

*Federal Register*. (1981). Washington, DC: U.S. Government Printing Office.

Field, S. (1996). Self-determination instructional strategies for youth with learning disabilities: *Journal of Learning Disabilities*, 29, 40-52.

Fuchs, L.S., Fuchs, D., Hamlett, C.L. & Phillips, N.B. (1995). General educators' specialized adaptation for students with learning disabilities: *Exceptional Children*, 61, 440-459.

Gordon, M. & Keiser, S. (Eds.). (1998). Ac*commodations in higher education under the Americans with Disabilities Act.* NY, NY: The Guilford Press.

Graham, S., Schwartz, S., & MacArthur, C. (1993). Knowledge of writing and the composing process, attitude toward writing, self-efficacy for students with and without learning disabilities: *Journal of Learning Disabilities*, 26, 237-249.

Greenwood, J. (1983). Adapting a college preparatory curriculum for dyslexic adolescents: *Annals of Dyslexia*, 33, 235-242.

Gregg, N. & Ferri, B. (1998). Hearing voices, witnessing pain: in response to "why does my stomach hurt?": *Journal of Learning Disabilities*, 31, 517-19.

Guckenberger v. Boston University, 974 F. Supp. 106 (D. Massachusetts 1997).

Guterman, B. R. (1995). The validity of categorical learning disabilities services: The consumer's view: *Exceptional Children*, 62, 111-124.

Hagborg, W. (1999). Scholastic competence subgroups among high school students with learning disabilities: *Learning Disability Quarterly*, 22, 3-10.

Hoffman, A. & Field, S. (1995). Promoting self-determination through effective curriculum development: *Intervention in School & Clinic*, 30, 134.

Hamilton, S. & Hamilton, A. (1992). Mentoring programs: Promise and paradox: *Phi Delta Kappan*, 71, 546-551.

Houck, C.K., Engelhard J.B. & Geller, C.H. (1990). Special education supervisors' perceptions of secondary LD programs: A comparison with LD teachers' views: *Journal of Learning Disabilities*, 23, 320-324.

Hoy, C. & Manglitz, E. (1996). Social and affective adjustment of adults with learning disabilities: A life-span perspective. In G. Noel & C. Hoy (Eds.), *Adults with learning disabilities: Theoretical and practical perspectives.* (pp. 208-231). New York, NY, USA: The Guilford Press.

Individuals with Disabilities Education Act of 1990, 20 U.S.C. * 1400 et seq.

Kauffman, J. M. & Hallahan, D.P.(1981). *Handbook of Special Education*; Paramus: USA; Prentice Hall.

Kavale, K. & Forness, S. (1995). *The nature of learning disabilities: Critical elements of diagnosis and classification*. Mahwah, NJ: Lawrence Erlbaum Associates, Inc.

Klingner, J., Vaughn, S., Hughes, M., Schumm, J. & Elbaum, B. (1998). Outcomes for students with and without learning disabilities in inclusive classrooms: *Learning Disabilities Research & Practice*, 13, 153-161.

Kortering, L. & Braziel, P. (1999a). Staying in school: The perspective of ninth-grade students: *Remedial and Special Education*, 20, 106-13.

Kortering, L. & Braziel, P. (1999b). School dropout from the perspective of former students: implications for secondary special education programs: *Remedial and Special Education*, 20, 78-83.

Lenz, K., Schumaker, J., Deshler, D., Fuchs, D., Fuchs, L., Gordon, S., Morocco, C., Riley, M., Schumm J. & Vaughn, S. (1995). *Planning for academic diversity in America's classrooms: Windows on reality, research, change, and practice*. Lawrence, Kansas: Center for Research on Learning.

Lichtenstein, S. (1993). Transition from school to adulthood: Case studies of adults with learning disabilities who dropped out of school: *Exceptional Children*, 59, 336-47.

MacDonald, T. (1999). SSAD Simultaneous equations: Memory aiding mnemonics: *Mathematics in School*, 8, 13.

Mastropieri, M.A. & Scruggs, T.E. (1998). Enhancing school success with mnemonic strategies: *Intervention in School and Clinic*, 33, 201-8.

McIntosh, R., Vaughn, S., Schumm, J., Haager, D., & Lee, O. (1995). Observations of students with learning disabilities in the regular education classrooms: *Exceptional Children*, 60, 598-608.

Meltzer, L., Roditi, B., Houser, R. & Perlman M. (1998). Perceptions of academic strategies and competence in students with learning disabilities: *Journal of Learning Disabilities*, 31, 437-51.

Montague, M. (1998). Research on metacognition in special education. In T. E. Scruggs & M. A. Mastropieri (Eds.), *Advances in learning and behavioral disabilities, Vol. 12*. (pp. 151-183). Greenwich, CT, USA: Jai Press, Inc.

Morocco, C., Riley, M., & Gordon, S. (1995). The elusive individual in teachers' planning. In G. Brannigan (Ed.), *The enlightened educator: Research adventures in the schools*. (pp. 154-176.). New York: McGraw-Hill.

O'Neill, M.E. & Douglas, V. I. (1991). Study strategies and story recall in attention deficit disorder and reading disability: *Journal of Abnormal Child Psychology*, 19(6), 671-692.

Patton, J. R., & Polloway, E. A. (Eds.). (1996). *Learning disabilities: The challenges of adulthood*. Austin, TX: Pro-Ed.

Pressley, M., Harris, K., & Guthrie, J. (Eds). (1992). *Promoting academic competence and literacy in school*. San Diego, CA, USA: Academic Press, Inc.

Putnam, M. L. (1992a). Characteristics of questions on tests administered by mainstream secondary classroom teachers: *Learning Disabilities Research & Practice*, 7, 129-136.

Putnam, M. L. (1992b). The testing practices of mainstream secondary classroom teachers: *Remedial and Special Education*, 13, 11-21.

Riley, M. K. (1983). Learning models and interventions. *Cognitive assessment for a broader-based remedial curriculum for children and adolescents with disabilities*. Paper presented at the 60th Annual Meeting of the American Orthopsychiatric Association Conference, Boston.

Riley, M. K. (1995). Alternative assessment provides the opportunity for students with learning disabilities to show they really do know: *Journal of the Learning Disabilities Association of Massachusetts*, 37, 1-9.

Riley, M. K. (1998). Leveling the playing field: Students with learning disabilities enjoying their competence, Working hard and having fun in college. In T. A. Citro, (Ed.), *The experts speak: Parenting the child with learning disabilities*. (pp.101-121). Boston: Learning Disabilities Association of Massachusetts.

Riley, M. K. (1999a). Keys to success in college for students with learning disabilities: Self-knowledge, self-advocacy, and individualized support services. In T. A. Citro, (Ed.), *Successful lifetime management for adults with learning disabilities*. (pp. 65-87). New York: Guilford Press.

Riley, M. K. (Author), & Citro, T. A. (Producer & Director). (1999b). *Pathways to success: College students with learning disabilities* [Videotape]. Boston: Ocean One Productions.

Riley, M. K. & Morocco, C. C. (1999). Talking in school: The role of constructivist conversation for written language. In M. Z. Fleishman, (Ed.), *The diagnostic teacher: Revitalizing professional development*. (pp. 104-132). New York: Teachers College Press.

Riley, M. K, Morocco, C. C., Gordon, S. M. & Howard, C. (1993). Walking the talk: Putting constructivist thinking into practice in classrooms: *Educational Horizons* 71(4), 187-196.

Rumelhart, D.E. (1980). Schemata: The building blocks of cognition. In R.J. Spiro, B.C. Bruce & W.F. Brewer (Eds.), *Theoretical issues in reading composition*. (pp.245-278). Hillsdale, NJ: Lawrence Erlbaum Associates.

Schumm , J., Vaughn, S., Haager, D., McDowell, J., Rothlein, L. & Saumell, L. (1995). General education teacher planning: What can students with learning disabilities expect?: *Exceptional Children*, 61, 335-352.

Scruggs,T. & Mastropieri, M. (1992a). Classroom applications of mnemonic instruction: acquisition, maintenance and generalization: *Exceptional Children*, 58, 219-231.

Scruggs, T. & Mastropieri, M. (1993). Special education for the twenty-first century: integrating learning strategies and thinking skills: *Journal of Learning Disabilities*, 26, 392-398.

Seidel, J. F. & Vaughn, S. (1991). Social alienation and the learning disabled school dropout: *Learning Disabilities Research & Practice*, 6, 152-157.

Silver, L. (Author), & Citro, T. A. (Producer & Director). (2000). *Portraits of success: Stories of hope and resilience* [Videotape]. Boston: Ocean One Productions.

Simmons, D., Kameenui, E. & Darch, C. (1988). The effect of textual proximity on fourth- and fifth-grade LD students' metacognitive awareness and strategic comprehension behavior: *Learning Disability Quarterly*, 11, 380-395.

Snow, J. (1992). Mental Flexibility and planning skills in children and adolescents with learning disabilities: *Journal of Learning Disabilities*, 25, 265-270.

Schumaker, J. & Deshler, D. (1998). Implementing the Regular Education Initiative in secondary schools: A different ball game: *Journal of Learning Disabilities*, 21, 36-42.

Shapiro, J. M. & Rich, R. (1999). *Facing learning disabilities in the adult years*. NY, NY: Oxford University Press.

Stephens, J. & Dwyer, F. (1997). Effect of varied mnemonics strategies in facilitating student achievement of different educational objectives: *International Journal of Instructional Media*, 24 (1), 75-88.

Swanson, H. L. (1990). Instruction derived from strategy deficit model: Overview of principles and procedures. In T. Scruggs & B. Y. L. Wong (Eds.), *Intervention research in learning disabilities*. (pp. 34-65). New York: Springer-Verlag.

Swanson, H. L., Carson, C. & Saches-Lee, C. (1996). A selective synthesis of intervention research for students with learning disabilities: *The School Psychology Review*, 25, 370-91.

Thomas, M. & Wang, A. (1996). Learning by the keyword mnemonic: Looking for long-term benefits: *Journal of Experimental Psychology*, 2, 330-342.

Torgesen, J. K. (1980). Conceptual and educational implications of the use of efficient task strategies by learning disabled children: *Journal of Learning Disabilities*, 13(7), 364-71.

U.S. Office of Special Education Programs (OSEP). (1995). *Improving the Individuals with Disabilities Education Act: IDEA reauthorization*. Washington, DC.

U.S. Office of Education. (1977). Assistance to states for education of Handicapped children: Procedures for evaluating specific learning disabilities. *Federal Register*, 42, 65082-65085.

Vaidya, S.R. (1999). Metacognitive learning strategies for students with learning disabilities: *Education*, 120, 186-9.

VanReusen, A.K. & Bos, C.S. (1990). IPLAN: Helping students communicate in planning conferences: *Teaching Exceptional Children*, 22, 30-32.

Vaughn, S. & Klingner, J.K. (1998). Students' perceptions of inclusion and resource room settings: *The Journal of Special Education*, 32, 79-88.

Vaughn, S., McIntosh, R., Schumm, J. & Haager, D. (1993). Social status, peer acceptance, and reciprocal friendships revisited: *Learning Disabilities Research & Practice*, 8, 82-88.

Vogel, S.A., & Adelman, P.B. (1992). The success of college students with learning disabilities: Factors related to educational attainment: *Journal of Learning Disabilities*, 25(7), 430-441.

Vogel, S.A., & Adelman, P.B. (1993). *Success for college students with learning disabilities: Factors related to educational attainments*. New York: Springer-Verlag.

Whinnery, K. (1992). College preparation for students with learning disabilities: A curriculum approach: *Preventing School Failure*, 37(1), 31-34.

Wickelgren, W. E. (1974). *How to solve problems*. San Francisco. CA: W. H. Freeman & Company.

Wong, B.Y.L., Wong, R., & Blenkinsop, J. (1989). Cognitive and metacognitive aspects of learning disabled adolescents' composing problems: *Learning Disability Quarterly*, 12, 300-22.

Wong, Bernice Y. L. (1999). Metacognition in writing. In R. Gallimore, L. P. Bernheimer, D. L. MacMillan, D. L. Speece, S. Vaughn (Eds.), *Developmental perspectives on children with high-incidence disabilities*. (pp. 183-198). Mahwah, NJ, USA: Lawrence Erlbaum Associates, Inc.

Wood, D., Bruner, J. S., Ross, G. (1976). The role of tutoring in problem solving: *Journal of Child Psychology & Psychiatry & Allied Disciplines*, 17(2), 89-100.

Zigmond, N. (1990). Rethinking secondary school programs for students with learning disabilities: *Focus on Exceptional Children*, 23, 1-22.

Zimmerman, B. J. (2000). Self-efficacy: An essential motive to learn: *Contemporary Educational Psychology*, 25(1), 82-91.

## Chapter 3 Rowley

American School Counselors Association. *Position statement: The school counselor and comprehensive guidance* [Adopted 1988 and revised 1993]. Alexandria, VA: Author.

Borders, L.D., & Drury, S.M. (1992). Comprehensive school counseling programs: A review for policymakers and practitioners: *Journal of Counseling and Development*, 70, 487-498.

Campbell, C.A., & Dahir, C.A. (1997). *Sharing the vision: The national standards for school counseling programs*. Alexandria, VA: National School Counselors Association.

Carns, A.W., & Carns, M.R. (1997). A systems approach to school counseling: *The School Counselor*, 44, 218-223.

Good, G.E., Fischer, A.R., Johnson, J.A., & Heppner, P.P. (1994). Norman C. Gysbers: A proponent of comprehensive school guidance programs: *Journal of Counseling and Development*, 73, 115-120.

Gysbers, N.C., & Henderson, P. (1994). *Developing and managing your school guidance program* (2nd ed.). Alexandria, VA: American School Counselors Association.

## Chapter 4 Guyer

Ferrett, S. (1994). *Peak Performance*. Burr Ridge, IL: Irwin Mirror Press.

Hallowell, E. & Ratey, J. (1994). *Driven to Distraction: Recognizing and Coping with Attention Deficit Disorder from Childhood through Adulthood.* New York: Pantheon Books.

Guyer, B. (1997). *The Pretenders: Gifted People Who Have Difficulty Learning.* Homewood, IL: High Tide Press.

Guyer, B. (Ed.). (2000). ADHD: *Achieving Success In School and In Life.* Boston: Allyn & Bacon, Inc.

Kravets, M. (1999). *The K&W Guide to Colleges for Students with Learning Disabilities or Attention Deficit Disorders: A Resource Book for Students, Parents, and Professionals.* New York: Random House.

Mangrum, C.(Ed.). (1997). *Peterson's Colleges: With Programs for Students with Learning Disabilities or Attention Deficit Disorders.* Princeton, NJ: Peterson's, Inc.

Parker, H. (1996). *The ADD Hyperactivity Handbook for Schools: Effective Strategies for Identifying and Treating Students with Attention Deficit Disorders in Elementary and Secondary Schools.* Plantation, FL: Specialty Press, Inc.

Stoner, J.; Farrell, M. & Guyer, B. (1997). *College: How Students with Dyslexia Can Maximize the Experience.* Baltimore: The International Dyslexia Association.

## Chapter 6 Hagin

HEATH Resource Center (Higher Education and Adult Training for People with Handicaps)

1 Dupont Circle, Washington, D.C. 20036
Publication: <u>Getting Ready for College</u>

Learning Disabilities Association of America (LDA)
4156 Library Road
Pittsburgh, PA 15234
Parent advocacy organization with state and local affiliates and a source for information, meetings and publications

National Council of Independent Living Programs
211 Wilson Boulevard Suite 405
Arlington, VA 2210
Source of information on independent living facilities

## Chapter 7 Glines

Levine, A., and Cureton, J., (1998). *When Hope and Fear Collide. A Portrait of Today's College Student.* San Francisco: Jossey Bass Publishers.

Elkind, D., (1984). *All Grown Up and No Place to Go: Teenagers in Crisis.* Boulder, Colorado: Westview Press.

Elkind, D., (1981). *The Hurried Child.* Boulder, Colorado: Westview Press.

Raskin, Marshall H., Roberta J. Goldberg, Eleanor L. Higgings, and Kenneth L. Herman (1999). Patterns of Change and Predictors of Success in Individuals With Learning Disabilities: Results From a Twenty-Year Longitudinal Study. *Learning Disabilities Research & Practice*, 14(1), 35-49.

## Chapter 8 Kline

Harvey, V. S. (1995). Interagency collaboration: Providing a system of care for students. *Special Services in the Schools*, *10*, 165-181.

Knackendoffel E. A., Robinson, S. M., Deshler, D. D., & Schumaker, J. B. (1992). *Collaborative problem solving: A step by step guide to creating educational solutions.* Lawrence, KS: Edge Enterprises, Inc.

Office of Superintendent of Public Instruction (OSPI). (February, 1998). *Special education and the law: A legal guide of families and educators.* Olympia: OSPI.

Seeger, K., & Aceves, J. Assisting with the school placement and interventions for children with special needs—from disabled to gifted. *Primary Care*, *22,* 51-68.

Skrtic, T. M., & Sailor, W. (1996). School-linked services integration: Crisis and opportunity in the transition to postmodern society. *Remedial Education*, *17*, 271-283.

Turnbull, H. R. (1993). *Free appropriate public education: The law and children with disabilities*. 4th. Ed. Denver, CO: Love Publishing Co.

## Chapter 10 Pisha

Meyer, A., Pisha, B., Murray, E., & Rose, D. (In Press). More than words: Learning to write in the digital world, in A. Bain, L. Baillet, & L. Moats (eds) *Written Language Disorders: Theory Into Practice,* 2nd Edition. PRO-ED, 8700 Shoal Creek Boulevard, Austin, Texas.

Meyer, A., Pisha, B., & Rose, D. (1991). Process and Product in Writing: Computer as Enabler, in A. Bain, L. Baillet, & L. Moats (eds) *Written Language Disorders: Theory Into Practice*. PRO-ED, 8700 Shoal Creek Boulevard, Austin, Texas.

Pisha, B. & Meyer, A. (July 1998) Smart Uses of the Smart Machine: Computers and your Child's Learning, *GAZETTE, The Journal of the Learning Disabilities Association of Massachusetts.*

Pisha, B. (1993). *Rates of Development of Keyboarding Skills in Elementary School Aged Children With and Without Identified Learning Disabilities*, unpublished doctoral dissertation, Harvard University Graduate School of Education.

Rose, D., Meyer, A., & Pisha, B. (1994). Out of Print: Literacy in the Electronic Age, in N. J. Ellsworth, C. N. Hedley, & A. N. Baratta (eds), *Literacy: A Redefinition.* Hillsdale, NJ: Lawrence Erlbaum Associates.

# Other Books Edited by Teresa Allissa Citro

## Successful Lifetime Management:
## Adults with Learning Disabilities

"This volume is a road map for adults with learning disabilities regardless of what stage they are at in their journeys of navigating the obstacles and opportunities to Successful Lifetime Management."

## The Experts Speak:
## Parenting the Child with
## Learning Disabilities

"This distinguished group of authors presents a brilliant collection of articles. The multidisciplinary viewpoints, perspectives and strategies focus on academic, collaborative, social, psychological and family issues. *The Experts Speak* is an excellent resource for professionals, parents and everyone facing the daily challenges of learning and attentional differences."

# Videos Produced by Teresa Allissa Citro

## Einstein and Me: Talking About Learning Disabilities

Kids speak openly and honestly about:
- How they found out about their learning disability.
- The policies and people who made life difficult.
- People and programs that helped them cope.
- Their strengths and talents.
- Their futures.

## Meeting with Success: Tips for a Successful IEP

It's easy to find dozens of documents explaining the IEP process, but an IEP meeting can turn into an adversarial nightmare even if everybody involved understands the "rules and regulations." **It doesn't have to be this way!** In this upbeat and optimistic video, narrated by Dr. Jerome Schultz, you'll observe "real" parents, teachers, administrators and other specialists as they demonstrate *Tips for Meeting with Success.*

## Stop and Go Ahead with Success:  An integrated approach to helping children develop social skills

Friendships are critical for our sense of well being. This video offers practical solutions for teachers and parents on how to address the social problems children with learning disabilities in elementary school face. It demonstrates an integrated approach to teaching social skills as they arise throughout the school day. When parents, teachers and other adults work together to coach children on these skills, children become more confident and enter social situations anticipating SUCCESS.

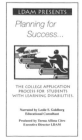

## Planning for Success: The College Application Process for Students with Learning Disabilities

In this video you will observe the college application process for one student with a learning disability. Individuals vary in strengths and weaknesses and yet all students have the ability to reach their full potential when carefully planning for success.

# Videos Produced by Teresa Allissa Citro

## Pathways to Success:
## College Students with Learning Disabilities

Students with learning disabilities share the strategies that have brought them success both at the graduate and undergraduate levels. They discuss the realities of adjusting to the new academic challenges and to the differences in support services between postsecondary and the high school levels.

## Profiles of Success: Successful Adults Achieving with Learning Disabilities

**Larry B. Silver** interviews young adults with learning disabilities about their experiences. In this video, meet three exceptional adults with learning disabilities who achieved success. Hear how they struggled and overcame obstacles and chose careers that best used their strengths. Let their stories of hope, fortitude and resilience encourage you. Dr. Silver goes on to explain what learning disabilities are and how teachers and parents can help every student with learning disabilities become "Profiles of Success."

## Portraits of Success: Fostering Hope and Resilience in Individuals with Learning Disabilities

This video features interviews by Larry B. Silver, M.D. and Robert Brooks, Ph.D. with adults, parents and teachers about their experiences with learning disabilities. These "Portraits of Success" will foster hope and resilience in children with learning disabilities.

# To Order Books or Videos
Please visit our website at www.LDAM.org
or call LDAM at 781-891-5009

# Join LDAM Today!

*LDAM is a non-profit, volunteer organization. Its financial support comes from membership dues, conference proceeds, grants and donations. LDAM policies are determined by elected officers and a Board of Directors.* Your contributions are greatly needed. **Contributions to LDAM are tax deductible.**

## Membership Includes

- Annual membership in Learning Disabilities Association of America and Learning Disabilities Association of Massachusetts
- Six LDA newsbrief publications.
- Tri-Annual issues of "The Journal of the Learning Disabilities Association of Massachusetts."
- Notification of conferences
- Reduced registration fees at conferences and workshops (including the International LDA Conference, Massachusetts regional LDA conferences, and the Joint Conference on Learning Disabilities)
- Information about resources and services pertaining to learning disabilities, "Yearly Directory on Learning Disabilities."
- New member packet information

## Membership Information

Name _____     Date _____

Address _____     ❏ Professional

City _____     ❏ Institutional

State/Zip _____     ❏ Student

Telephone _____     ❏ Adult

## Interests

**I am willing to work on the following committees:**

___ Public Relations   ___ Fund Raising
___ Multi Cultural     ___ Conferences
___ Grants             ___ Legislative
___ Development        ___ Speakers Bureau
___ Research and Dissemination
___ Educational (K-Post Secondary

**Please enroll me as a member of the Learning Disabilities Association of Massachusetts:** ___ New   ___ Renew

___ Individual (Family) $40.00
___ Professional $60.00
___ Foreign $65.00
___ Institutional $100
___ Tax Deductible Contribution _____

*Institutional members receive a 10% discount to exhibit at our conferences, a 10% discount for ads placed in the Gazette and pre-conference brochures, and unlimited attendance at member's fee to the conferences.*

Make checks payable to **LDAM.**
Send to **LDAM, P.O. Box 142, Weston, MA 02493** or
Register online at **www.LDAM.org**